Serving the Word

Serving the Word

Essays in Honor of Dr. Chuck Sackett

Edited by

Eddy Sanders

and

Frank Dicken

Foreword by

Tom Tanner

WIPF *&* STOCK · Eugene, Oregon

SERVING THE WORD
Essays in Honor of Dr. Chuck Sackett

Wipf & Stock
An Imprint of Wipf and Stock Publishers
199 W. 8th Ave., Suite 3
Eugene, OR 97401

www.wipfandstock.com

ISBN 13: 978-1-62564-979-9

Cataloguing-in-Publication Data

Sanders, Eddy, and Frank Dicken

    Serving the word: essays in honor of Chuck Sackett / Eddy Sanders and Frank Dicken.

    xvi + 180 p. ; 23 cm. Includes bibliographical references.

    ISBN 13: 978-1-62564-979-9

    1. Preaching

CALL NUMBER BV4211.S35

Manufactured in the U.S.A.   07/20/2015

Contents

Contributors

Frank Dicken (PhD), Assistant Professor of New Testament at Lincoln Christian University (Lincoln, IL)

J. Kent Edwards (PhD, DMin), Founder and CEO of CrossTalk Global; Professor of Preaching and Leadership at Talbot School of Theology, Biola University (La Mirada, CA)

David Fincher (PhD), President at Central Christian College of the Bible (Moberly, MO)

Dinelle Frankland (DWS), Academic Dean and Professor of Worship at Lincoln Christian Seminary (Lincoln, IL)

Don Green (DMin), President at Lincoln Christian University (Lincoln, IL)

Fred Hansen (PhD Candidate), Assistant Professor of Biblical Studies at TCM International Institute (Heiligenkreuz, Austria)

Jonathan Hughes (MA), Lead Minister at Grand Avenue Christian Church (Carbondale, IL)

J. K. Jones (DMin), Pastor of Spiritual Formation at Eastview Christian Church (Normal, IL); Professor at Large and Director of the MA Program in Spiritual Formation at Lincoln Christian University (Lincoln, IL)

Eddy Sanders (DMin), Professor of Biblical Studies and Ministry at Saint Louis Christian College (Florissant, MO)

Mark Scott (DMin), Professor of New Testament and Director of the Preaching Department at Ozark Christian College (Joplin, MO)

Mark Searby (DMin), Director of Doctor of Ministry Studies at Beeson Divinity School (Birmingham, AL)

Tom Tanner (PhD), Director of Accreditation and Institutional Evaluation at The Association of Theological Schools (Pittsburgh, PA)

Tony Twist (PhD, DMin), President of TCM International Institute (Heiligenkreuz, Austria)

Brooks Wilson (ThM), Senior Minister at South Side Christian Church (Springfield, IL)

Neal Windham (DMin), Professor of Christian Spirituality at Lincoln Christian University (Lincoln, IL)

Foreword
Two Texts That Testify to One Preacher

Tom Tanner

Two texts, for me, testify to the life and legacy of Glenn Charles Sackett. The first is an Old Testament text from one of Chuck's favorite chapters—Isaiah 40. The second is a New Testament text from one of my favorite chapters—Acts 20. In this preface to a volume about hermeneutics and homiletics, allow me to interpret very personally how these two texts speak volumes about this preacher and his preaching.

The first text is from Isaiah 40:31

It could be tattooed on Chuck's forehead—if he would ever tolerate a tattoo. "Those who hope in the Lord will renew their strength. . . . they will run and not grow weary" (NIV). It is a text that testifies to the character and charisma of this humble man of God who lives and loves the Word of God. This text is a runner's text—and Chuck is a runner, a long-distance runner, a veteran of many marathons, including the Boston Marathon three times over. But most of the marathons he has run in his life have not been on a race course; they have been run on a life course that spans sixty-plus years (I should know; Chuck and I were born only four days apart). His life course has been a marathon of ministry that has taken him from the West

Coast to the East Coast in his preaching and teaching. It has been a missionary course that has taken him from North America to Eastern Europe in his travels. It has been a spiritual journey that has taken him from the son of a saloon keeper to the sinner saved by grace—and impatient to share that grace with anyone and everyone.

To be sure, a long-distance runner has to be a patient person, and Chuck is a patient person—most of the time. He is not impatient nor impetuous nor impulsive, unless he sees a need that requires God's grace. Then he can be very impatient and very impetuous and very impulsive. He is the kind of teacher who would impetuously—and literally—throw the book at you (in this case, a hymnbook) if he thought you needed that to help you learn an important life lesson (ask one of his students from years ago). He is the kind of traveling companion who would impulsively walk past scores of people waiting in line for hours at O'Hare in order to ask an airline agent if he could find a seat on a delayed flight for him and his friend (that would be me), so that we would not miss our planned teaching trip to Haus Edelweiss. And we got our seats (first class, no less—and for no more) because Chuck struck up a pastoral conversation with an airline agent and learned that he was from the same country where Chuck had recently preached in Eastern Europe—just another example of Chuck's ability to turn any marathon into a ministry, even in an airport line. He is the kind of preacher who, despite his introversion, can preach his heart out and sometimes impatiently so—whether before thousands at the North American Christian Convention or before a few freshmen venturing out on their own faith for the first time—almost begging his hearers for a hearing about God's gospel of grace. All so that they can experience the same kind of grace that he has experienced. Chuck has run patiently his life's marathon for sixty some years and he has "not grown weary" because "his hope is in the Lord."

The second text is from Acts 20:20

It gives us 20/20 vision into the passion of the preacher we honor in this book. "You know that I have not hesitated to preach anything that would be helpful to you, but have taught you publicly and from house to house." This passage is part of Paul's farewell to the Ephesian elders. It's an unusual text about preaching—a very personal text. It's the only speech of Paul recorded in the book of Acts that was delivered to Christians, to very dear friends of Paul. It's the only recorded speech of Paul the apostle in the Acts of the Apostles that was so emotional it ended in praying and hugging, in kissing and crying. It's just an unusually personal passage about preaching. And it gives us some insight into the preaching and person of this man we honor.

Most of those reading this book know about Dr. Sackett's public preaching and teaching. He began publicly teaching preaching at Lincoln Christian University in 1983, more than 30 years ago. He has also taught preaching publicly at Beeson Divinity School in Alabama and at TCM International Institute in Austria. He has preached publicly in southern Illinois, in coastal Oregon, and in his home state of Idaho—or as he calls it, the promised land. And that list does not even include countless other places where he has preached when asked and when not preaching at Madison Park Christian Church in Quincy, Illinois, where he has served since 1998. He has even been a presenter and president for the Evangelical Homiletics Society. In short, he is one of the most public and well-known preachers among the churches of the Stone-Campbell movement, even chosen as a keynote speaker for the North American Christian Convention. He has spoken God's grace to one thousand in a convention hall, but also to just one in a coffee house. And that highlights an important part of this passage: "I have taught you publicly *and from house to house.*" It's the nonpublic, personal, private, house-to-house part of Chuck's preaching that intrigues me most.

While many may know about Dr. Sackett's public preaching, most may not know about his preaching and teaching "from house to house." You may not know how he came to my house late one Friday night many years ago and stood with me when it appeared that I was about to lose my ministry and whispered in my ear these four words of grace, "You go, I go." You may not know how he came unasked to the house of J. K. and Sue Jones (two of his LCU faculty colleagues) very early one winter morning during a near blizzard and shoveled their driveway so they could take their daughter to emergency eye care surgery. He preached a sermon that day, not with a shout but with a shovel. You may not know how he has taught from house to house for decades at Haus Edelweiss in Austria, how quietly and humbly he has taught these students from Eastern Europe—in their classrooms, in their living rooms, in their dining rooms, and even over the Haus kitchen sink doing dishes. You may not know how he has taught the word of God in his own house, testifying to God's grace with his wife, Gail, to their three daughters—and now to two sons-in-law who have followed him in his ministry of preaching and teaching. "Publicly and from house to house," Chuck Sackett has preached God's grace as a sinner saved by grace.

I know I said two texts typify Chuck for me. Let me sneak in a third before I close—one that ties the first two together. Just before Paul tearfully tells his dear friends in Acts 20:25 that "none of you among whom I have gone about preaching the kingdom will ever see me again," he shares with them in the preceding verse this telling summary of his life's work: "I consider my life worth nothing to me, if only I may finish the race and complete the task the Lord Jesus has given me—the task of testifying to the gospel of God's grace." Paul said that. Chuck lives that. I'm reminded of the words of the famous runner turned missionary, Eric Liddell, in *Chariots of Fire*: "I believe God made me for a purpose, but he also made me fast. And when I run, I feel His pleasure." God made Chuck Sackett for a purpose, and when he preaches, we all feel God's pleasure.

Introduction

EDDY SANDERS AND FRANK DICKEN

SEVERAL HELPFUL BOOKS HAVE been published in recent years addressing hermeneutics and homiletics.[1] Haddon Robinson's ever-popular *Biblical Preaching* is in its third edition.[2] These books address hermeneutics and homiletics from a methodological perspective. On the other hand, Haddon Robinson and Craig Brian Larson's *The Art & Craft of Biblical Preaching* addresses issues of hermeneutics and homiletics from a separatist approach.[3] Issues are addressed independently rather than woven into the fabric of an author's homiletical approach. The present volume addresses hermeneutics and homiletics in the same vein as *The Art & Craft of Biblical Preaching*—from an independent approach.

The present volume also addresses these issues in honor of Dr. Chuck Sackett for his faithful service to the kingdom of God both as a preacher and a teacher of preachers. Chuck's influence in the field and practice of hermeneutics and homiletics is substantial. If one picks up a copy of Don Sunukjian's *Invitation to Biblical Preaching*, he or she will notice Chuck's name on the back cover. Sackett writes that *Invitation to Biblical Preaching*

---

1. Carter et al., *Preaching God's Word*; Chapell, *Christ-Centered Preaching*, 2nd ed.; Edwards, *Effective First-Person Biblical Preaching*; Sunukjian, *Invitation to Biblical Preaching*; Akin, Curtis, and Rummage, *Engaging Exposition*.

2. Robinson, *Biblical Preaching*, 3rd ed.

3. Robinson and Larson, eds., *The Art & Craft of Biblical Preaching*.

"will take its rightful place among the homiletics textbooks of our class-rooms and in the stacks of refreshing readings for experienced pastors."[4] Something similar can be said of Chuck Sackett: he has taken his rightful place among interpreters, preachers, and Christian ministers and his wide-spread influence is refreshing for experienced and inexperienced pastors. This volume seeks to honor Chuck with a variety of essays focused upon the tasks of interpretation and proclamation from his students, colleagues, friends, and family.

The volume begins with David Fincher exploring Augustine's ap-proach to troublesome passages. Fincher first outlines Augustine's herme-neutical approach called "charity criticism" and then applies that approach to Exodus 32. Fincher suggests that although charity criticism should not become a default method for preaching, it may serve as an ancient model for interpretation in a culture that shows hostility towards the Bible.

Frank Dicken's essay "New Testament Narrative Criticism and the Preacher: The Beginning of a Discussion" offers an application of New Testament narrative criticism for preachers. His explanation of narrative criticism will assist the preacher in preparation through attention to the perspective of the implied reader. The key in preparation, Dicken argues, is *plot* as the driving force rather than a basic element to receive attention in exegetical analysis.

"The Speeches in Acts as a Rhetoric of Relevance," written by Neal Windham, is the third essay. Windham argues that the speeches in Acts pos-sess a model for relevant preaching. The preacher discovers relevance when he or she analyzes the speeches through Windham's "theoretical matrix."

Following this is J. Kent Edwards's essay that offers a strategy for "Transformational Preaching." Utilizing the educational theories of Jack Mezirow, Edwards argues for the need for transformational preaching and a strategy for the preacher to achieve transformational preaching. His strat-egy is found in a multilayered comparison that invites the preacher and listener into the plot and the protagonist's struggle in the biblical text.

Eddy Sanders's article, "A General Topic as Part of Biblical Preach-ing's Hermeneutical Methodology" argues that a general topic should be included in hermeneutical methodologies. Sanders explores how a general topic in biblical studies and speech communication is utilized and offers an example of a sermon that effectively employs a general topic.

---

4. Sunukjian, *Invitation to Biblical Preaching*, back cover.

Jonathan Hughes's "The Perpetrator and the Preacher: It's Sunday, Can You Come Out and Play?" offers two paradigms (Frames and Suspicion) that inhibit effective sermons. His suggestion is an approach to preaching that "requires deep study of Scripture in order to help the congregation see how their life fits into the comedy of Scripture." Using J. William Whedee's four characteristics of comedy, Hughes offers interpreters and preachers tremendous possibilities for effective and creative communication.

Following this is "Microscope and Telescope: How Expositional Preaching Grows Into Theological Arc" by Mark Scott. In this essay, Scott explains the image of the "theological arc" and offers nine characteristics of preaching. These characteristics will ensure sermons are Christ-centered, expository, and communicate Scripture's overarching narrative.

The next article, Mark Searby's "Staying in the Text—Preaching to the Heart," offers the preacher assistance where many struggle: a bridge between head and heart. Mark Searby attempts to bridge this gap in sermons through a model for theological reflection. Searby's model keeps the Holy Spirit at the center of the preaching task and event with emphasis upon Scripture, tradition, experience, and culture.

The next article addresses the challenges between preaching and worship, between preacher and worship leader. Dinelle Frankland observes in "The Reciprocity of Preaching and Worship" that worship "has had an oddly distant relationship with preaching." She addresses this distance through an insightful discussion between preaching and worship—and their leaders and proponents—that requires mutual respect. Frankland reminds preachers that the congregation looks to the preacher as a leader. Worship must be an integral part of the preacher's life and leadership for them to tell the gospel story in Sunday gatherings.

J.K. Jones's article "The Preacher as the Lead Student" reminds preachers that they are students. Specifically, they are the lead student and that reality has expectations outside of Sunday morning. Exploring one key text from the Old Testament and one from the New Testament, Jones offers stirring biblical examples that should remain a part of the preacher's study life. Through intense and diligent study, Jones suggests, the preacher remains in sacred partnership with the King of the universe.

The important topic of a multigenerational audience is addressed in "What Do You Do with All This Snow? Shaping a Sermon in a Multigenerational Context" by Brooks Wilson. Using the images of snow and snowman building, Wilson explores generational differences and the means by which a preacher can effectively address those differences.

Tony Twist and Fred Hansen shift the perspective to Eastern Europe where effective interpretation and presentation require humility and cultural sensitivity. Their article, "Multicultural Preaching and Teaching in Eastern Europe," explore how multicultural communication benefits from an increased CQ, or cultural intelligence. Based on the work of Soon Ang and Linn Van Dyne, Hansen and Twist offer insights for multicultural communication, as opposed to cross-cultural communication, that allow for effective communication of Scripture's message.

Lincoln Christian University's president, Don Green, concludes the essays with an article that positions the previous essays in their rightful place: effective church leadership through preaching. Green's article, "Leading a Congregation through Preaching," reminds preachers that various hermeneutical and homiletical issues are best utilized when they effectively lead a church. Green offers an example of a leader that he believes is effectively leading a church through preaching.

The essays compiled in this book are a small sampling of contemporary hermeneutical and homiletical issues impacting the church and preachers. We hope this volume is useful to the beginning preacher and the seasoned preacher alike.

A special thanks is due to the leadership of Madison Park Christian Church in Quincy, IL, who helped make this volume possible.

Augustine's Approach to Preaching Problematic Passages

David Fincher

Introduction to Charity Criticism

AUGUSTINE OF HIPPO (354–430), appointed to be a bishop in 395, was one of the most prolific writers of the church fathers. He is best known for writing the *Confessions*, an extremely personal devotional work completed in 397, and *The City of God*, a voluminous theological treatise written from 413–426. But before the *Confessions*, Augustine started work in 397 on a technical book entitled *De Doctrina Christiana, iv libri* (*On Christian Doctrine, in four books*). After completing almost all of the first three books, Augustine put the work aside for thirty years, after which he finished book three and added book four in 426.[1]

Augustine made the goal of *On Christian Doctrine* clear in the preface. He wanted Christians to be able to understand the "secrets of the sacred writings" through rules of interpretation he would teach them. This chapter presents the method Augustine proposed for understanding and teaching

1. At least four issues of *Christian History* magazine have focused significantly on Augustine's life and works. *St. Augustine of Hippo* (issue 15), *St. Augustine: Sinner, Bishop, Saint* (issue 67), *The First Bible Teachers* (issue 80), and *Building the City of God in a Crumbling World* (issue 94).

Scripture, which I call "charity criticism."[2] It provides a clear path for a speaker to find the most preachable points in a text, especially in problematic passages.

On several occasions, Augustine refers to the twofold love (*charitas*) that should guide all Christians: love for God and love for neighbor. He then points out that the goal of understanding Scripture is to help Christians accomplish charity. He writes,

> Whoever, then, thinks that he understands the Holy Scriptures, or any part of them, but puts such an interpretation upon them as does not tend to build up this twofold love of God and our neighbor, does not yet understand them as he ought. If, on the other hand, a man draws a meaning from them that may be used for the building up of love . . . he is wholly clear from the charge of deception. (1.36.40)[3]

Augustine will repeat often the theme of charity. It is the center of his plan for interpreting Scripture. Because the Scripture is given by God to build up love, then the proper interpretation will lead to love for neighbor and God. He writes that students must "fully understand that 'the end of the commandment is charity, out of a pure heart'" (1.40.44). This gives a clear goal for a preacher to find meaning and speak to an audience.

Assumptions of Charity Criticism

Much of book one describes the definitional assumptions of doctrine. As early as 1.5.5, Augustine discusses the Trinity, a key theological concept for him. He continues in book one to describe the nature of God, how the Word became flesh, and the way to salvation. He speaks of the church, death and resurrection, and the key doctrine of practical theology, the twofold love for God and neighbor (1.26.27). Augustine assumes that the student of Scripture will try to interpret within the parameters of good theology. For his purposes, nontheological interpretation is pointless.

Apparently, some Christians were reluctant to use nonsacred ("profane") sources to better understand Scripture. Augustine believes that all knowledge can be helpful in approaching Scripture and writes, "Let every good and true Christian understand that wherever truth may be found,

2. For a brief introduction to this concept see Bray, "Augustine's Key," 42–44.

3. Augustine, *On Christian Doctrine*, http://www.ccel.org/a/augustine/doctrine/.

it belongs to his Master" (2.18.28). In contrast to those who would try to understand Scripture by waiting for God to speak to them, Augustine encouraged the usage of history (2.28), natural science (2.29), mechanical arts (2.30), dialectics (2.31), laws of inference (2.33), rules of eloquence (2.36), and rhetoric (2.37).

Regarding Scripture, Augustine admits that a passage can have unknown or ambiguous "signs." He writes, "Now there are two causes which prevent what is written from being understood: its being veiled either under unknown, or under ambiguous signs. Signs are either proper or figurative" (2.10.15). "Unknown signs" are far easier to understand than the ambiguous. The proper, or unknown, signs are those that an interpreter is ignorant of but can easily find more information about. Some of these words come from other languages and can be understood by consulting someone who knows the language. Other unknown signs are simply unknown because the interpreter is unfamiliar with their meaning.

Book three describes "ambiguous signs," words that should be interpreted symbolically instead of literally. Augustine describes several barriers that must be removed in order to understand figurative language and devises a system that allowed an interpreter to discern both historic value and symbolic meaning in a text. The author's intended meaning, even if figurative, could become clear without establishing the text as fictional.

A key assumption in Augustine is that a passage can have either obscure or clear signs. There are many passages of Scripture that are not immediately understandable. By understanding, Augustine means arriving at "the meaning the writer intended" (3.27.38). There are some passages in which that meaning is easier to find. But if an interpreter is struggling to understand a passage, finding another biblical passage with similar teaching may unlock the meaning of the obscure passage. Augustine assumes that this is the provision of God through the Holy Spirit, so that readers would be able to understand Scripture.

> If a man in searching the Scriptures endeavors to get at the intention of the author through whom the Holy Spirit spoke . . . he is free from blame so long as he is supported by the testimony of some other passage of Scripture. . . . The Holy Spirit . . . foresaw that this interpretation would occur to the reader, nay, made provision that it should occur to him. (3.27.38)

Theoretically, every difficult passage of Scripture should be able to be explained with a clearer passage. Despite that, Augustine still gives a process for understanding those difficult passages.

To summarize *On Christian Doctrine*, Augustine proposes that a doctrinally orthodox Christian who desires to promote love for God and neighbor can use various forms of knowledge and reason to arrive at the author's intended meaning for the signs in the text. These signs must be understood and taught, by allowing difficult passages to be explained by clearer passages.

Process of Charity Criticism

The primary goal of Augustine's interpretive method is to understand figurative passages. After the passage has been found and identified in the canon, the interpreter should gain familiarity with the text.[4] A preacher will read the passage often enough to commit it to memory. He says, "The first rule to be observed is, as I said, to know these books, if not yet with the understanding, still to read them so as to commit them to memory, or at least so as not to remain wholly ignorant of them" (2.9.14). The interpreter must also find an accurate version (translation) of the text. Augustine writes, "The great remedy for ignorance of proper signs is knowledge of languages" (2.11.16). He warns that there are times that a translator is "deceived by an ambiguity in the original language, and puts upon the passage a construction that is wholly alien to the sense of the writer" (2.12.18). Augustine's method requires a text within the canon, familiarity with the text in question, and access to the original language or a reliable translation.

The second part of the method of charity criticism is to find and explain the unknown signs of a passage. Augustine breaks these unknown signs down into places an interpreter's ignorance may hide the text's meaning. Three unknown signs to discover are names, nature, and numbers.[5]

Many signs in Scripture have meaning based on their figurative *names*. Augustine lists names such as Adam, Eve, Abraham, Moses, Jerusalem,

---

4. Augustine elucidates the books that make up the canon of Scripture in 2.8.13. In 2.8.12, he explains that a book is canonical if the greater number of churches and the churches that have the greater authority have accepted it.

5. He also addressed the unknown sign of music in 2.16.26, but it refers to the rare mention of musical instruments and the poetic quality of the original text, which is beyond the scope of the interpreter he was attempting to equip.

Sinai, and Siloam as examples of signs that can be better interpreted by knowing the meaning of the name (2.16.23). He refers interpreters to those men skilled in language who can explain what names mean. He writes, "When these names have been investigated and explained, many figurative expressions in Scripture become clear" (2.16.23).

Other signs in Scripture are obscured by an ignorance of things in *nature.* These include animals, minerals, or plants that might be mentioned in a text. Because Scripture uses everyday items to explain spiritual truths, it benefits an interpreter to have detailed knowledge of those items. Augustine uses hyssop, a plant referred to in Scripture, as an example of this. He writes, "Many, again, by reason of their ignorance of hyssop, not knowing the virtue it has in cleansing the lungs, nor the power it is said to have of piercing rocks with its roots, although it is a small and insignificant plant, cannot make out why it is said, 'purge me with hyssop, and I shall be clean'" (2.16.24). He also refers to animals and minerals that need a clear understanding, such as the serpent and beryl.

Another sign in Scripture of which many people are ignorant is *numbers.* A true interpreter will want to know the spiritual meaning of numbers, such as the forty days that Moses, Elijah, and Jesus spent fasting. Augustine explains the meaning of forty by looking to the components of forty: ten (fullness of knowledge) times four (fullness of time). He summarizes, "Many other numbers and combinations of numbers are used in the sacred writings, to convey instruction under a figurative guise, and ignorance of numbers often shuts out the reader from this instruction" (2.16.25). The allegorical interpretation of numbers was quite popular in Augustine's time, and he believed that it was possible to assign a spiritual meaning to every number in the Bible.

The ability to overcome the ignorance of these unknown signs will prepare the interpreter to have a proper understanding of Scripture. But a more difficult task is to examine and solve its ambiguities. According to Augustine, ambiguity lies in determining whether a word is proper or metaphorical. He writes, "The chief thing to be inquired into, therefore, in regard to any expression that we are trying to understand is, whether it is literal or figurative" (3.24.34). He says many people are slaves to taking Scripture literally, a practice that must be avoided.[6] Augustine's book does not give a guide to determining what the figurative meaning of a passage is

6. Augustine states, "We must beware of taking a figurative expression literally" (3.5.9).

as much as it points out the occasion when a figurative meaning is necessary. The overarching principle for determining figurative language comes back to Augustine's "charity criticism." His main concern is that the Bible will be used to promote love for God and love for neighbor. Therefore, it follows that:

> Whatever there is in the word of God that cannot, when taken literally, be referred either to purity of life or soundness of doctrine, you may set down as figurative. Purity of life has reference to the love of God and one's neighbor; soundness of doctrine to the knowledge of God and one's neighbor. (3.10.14)

Stated negatively, the interpreter is to avoid any literal interpretation that will hinder love from being practiced. Stated positively, Augustine writes, "In regard to figurative expressions, a rule such as the following will be observed, to carefully turn over in our minds and meditate upon what we read till an interpretation be found that tends to establish the reign of love" (3.15.23). Either way, love is seen as the primary guide for interpretation.

On several occasions, Augustine says a literal interpretation will hinder an interpreter from love. Those passages that seem to ascribe severity to God and the saints must be understood figuratively (3.11.17). Sayings and actions which are ascribed to God and the saints, and which seem to be wicked to the unskillful, must also be carefully considered for figurative meaning (3.12.18). If a command in the Scripture "seems to enjoin a crime or vice, or to forbid an act of prudence or benevolence, it is figurative" (3.16.24). An example Augustine gives is Romans 12:20: "If your enemies are hungry, feed them; if they are thirsty, give them something to drink; for by doing this you will heap burning coals on their heads." Obviously, the first section is to be interpreted literally, for that would demonstrate love for a neighbor. The second section, however, must be interpreted figuratively, for it would not be loving to heap coals of fire on the head of a person. Augustine gives various other examples, but the point is still the same. If Scripture's purpose is to promote love, a literal interpretation that does otherwise must be abandoned for a figurative interpretation.

The most specific instruction that Augustine gives for understanding obscure passages can be found at 3.26ff., where Augustine describes what has been called the *analogy of Scripture*. This says that by looking for teaching in the literal passages of Scripture, the obscure passages can then be adequately explained so that the Bible does not contradict itself, but rather explains itself. In fact, he is satisfied with conflicting interpretations of the same passage, as long as both interpretations can be found to be present in another Scripture. He writes,

> When . . . two or more interpretations are put upon the same words of Scripture, even though the meaning the writer intended remain undiscovered, there is no danger if it can be shown from other passages of Scripture that any of the interpretations put on the words is in harmony with the truth. (3.27.38)

Augustine holds out the chance that passages of Scripture may not have a clear explanation from other sources. In those cases, he admits that the best a student can do is appeal to the *evidence of reason*, which he describes as "a dangerous practice" (3.28.39). However, most ambiguous signs can be discovered through looking at the rest of Scripture.

Through these three general steps, the reader is presented with Augustine's charity criticism, the author's intended meaning is discovered as it promotes love of neighbor and love for God. By establishing the text within the canon and in an accurate version, overcoming the barriers of unknown signs, and identifying passages which must be interpreted figuratively, the meaning of Scripture necessary for preaching and teaching is uncovered.[7]

Evaluation of Charity Criticism

Several downfalls prevent it from being a default method for preaching and teaching every text, but it does provide some opportunities to gain insight. Although this system is intended for figurative passages, we may ask why it cannot be applied to literal passages. Augustine assumes a text with no figurative aspects can be properly understood. But even literal passages need careful thought in order to determine intended meaning.

We may also rightly ask if this method masks important meanings and themes other than love. By establishing charity as the primary lens through which Scripture is interpreted, Augustine may have filtered out the interpretation of other important meanings and themes. It is possible that every passage (literal or figurative) has a point to be made about love for God and neighbor. However, it would be monotonous if every sermon made the point of loving God and loving our neighbor, even if it is the most

---

7. Book four discusses the second half of Augustine's theory, which is that of preaching, or making known the knowledge gained through interpretation. Although his words are insightful for those studying public speaking or preaching, they are not as relevant for the practice of rhetorical criticism, and are not included in this chapter.

important command. While love might be the most important meaning of Scripture as a whole, it is not necessarily the most important meaning of a text. The greatest virtue may be love, but it is not the only virtue.

The greatest weakness of this method of understanding Scripture may be the apparent contradiction between finding the author's intended meaning and finding an allegorical meaning. For instance, he uses the example from Song of Solomon, written about the woman's teeth being like a flock of sheep that are shorn which come up from the washing (1.6.7). He interprets the teeth to be the holy men of the church who "tear men away from their errors and bring them into the church's body." It is doubtful that Solomon had such a meaning in mind when he wrote this passage in a book that so clearly refers to the physical love between a man and his bride. The most obvious explanation is that he was complimenting her beautiful teeth! Even more, no other passage of Scripture calls men "teeth." Therefore, it seems that Augustine is appealing to reason alone, which he himself calls "a dangerous practice" (3.28.39).

Numerous examples of a forced interpretation exist, protected by his statement that "if his mistaken interpretation tends to build up love" (1.36.41), he gets to the right place. That seems to be another way of saying "the ends justify the means," a principle that should not guide the interpretation of Scripture.

With those negatives in mind, it should be mentioned that there are some benefits to this methodology. It is extremely helpful in dealing with difficult passages that might be disputed. As a former pagan, Augustine knew the kinds of attacks formulated against the Bible. His plan for interpreting the Bible would disarm some of those before they could be executed. As we will see later, there are many passages regarding human suffering, God's judgment, or man's poor behavior that might be difficult to preach positively from. Augustine's approach provides a way to speak positively about a negative text.

His approach was extremely practical for the untrained Christian teacher, the person most likely to have used it. The emphasis on charity seems especially useful for sermons and devotions, the most practical applications of scriptural interpretation in this time period. Bray writes, "His real contribution is that he offered a key to interpreting Scripture that unlocked the Bible's riches for even the unlearned reader."[8] Christians who

---

8. Bray, "Augustine's Key," 43.

practiced this would find themselves with a better understanding of the "secrets" of the Scripture and the ability to share them with others.

Application of Charity Criticism to Exodus 32

In the remainder of this chapter, I will apply charity criticism to Exod 32, a significant chapter in the Hebrew Bible. Various writers have approached the text from historical and cultural perspectives, seeking to help the reader understand the backgrounds and contexts of the passage. They have explored cultural meanings of the different aspects of the narrative.[9] Another author has explained theological significances of the different actions.[10] Two authors have reconstructed the development of the literary text from a variety of proposed sources.[11]

But Exod 32 is a very difficult text for Christians to preach from, because Moses instructs the Levites (priests) to kill every one of their friends who are engaging in idolatry. Not only that, but the Levites themselves go throughout the camp with their swords, not afraid to bear the sword against their brothers. Because of such severity, this passage is difficult to harmonize with the promotion of love, Augustine's stated goal of interpretation and preaching.

Context and Background of Exodus 32

According to the book of Exodus, the Israelites spent several hundred years in Egypt after Joseph, a high-ranking official in Pharaoh's court, invited his brothers and their families to live in Egypt during a famine in the land of Palestine. In Exod 12:51, God used Moses and his brother Aaron to lead the people out of Egypt and towards the land God had promised them. The people were enthusiastic about leaving Egypt until they got to the desert and worried about food and water. The people often grumbled against Moses and Aaron (Exod 15:24; 16:2, 7; 17:3).

9. Aberbach and Smolar, "Aaron, Jeroboam, and the Golden Calves," 129–140; Oswalt, "Golden Calves," 13–20; Sasson, "Bovine Symbolism," 380–87; Lewy, "Story of the Golden Calf," 318–322; Perdue, "Golden Calf—A Reply," 237–246; Key, "Traces of the Worship," 20–26.

10. Faur, "Biblical Idea of Idolatry," 1–15.

11. Fensham, "Golden Calf and Ugarit," 191–93; Loewenstamm, "Making and Destruction," 481–490; Loewenstamm, "Golden Calf—A Rejoinder," 330–343.

During this time in the wilderness, God instructed Moses to come to the top of Mt. Sinai, where the tablets containing the Law would be given to him to take to the people (Exod 19). In Exod 32, they ask Aaron to construct a calf for their worship. When Moses discovers them worshipping the idol, he smashes the tablets (32:19), destroys the calf, and makes them drink the powdered gold (32:20). But when the people continue in their heathen activity, he calls for an army of priests to assemble and put to death those who are breaking God's commands (32:27). How can this text best be approached to bring devotional points that will encourage love? The following paragraphs show several ways the principles of Augustine's charity criticism are helpful.

Exod 32 refers to several *proper names* that can help us understand the passage. First, there is God, whose proper name appears thirteen times within the text (32:5, 7, 9, 11, 14, 26, 27, 29, 30, 31, 33, 35). Although the English translation is "Lord," God's covenant name has a very deep meaning. In Hebrew, the term means, "I Am" or "The one who is." This term is interpreted "I will be who/what I will be."[12] If God is the only one who by nature is and permanently exists, people reading this passage should love Him by not committing idolatry, as the Israelites did.

Another important name in the text is Moses, the main human character of the account. His name comes from the Egyptian word either meaning "extraction" or "a son."[13] The first meaning is most probable, as Exod 2:10 says that Pharaoh's daughter named him Moses, "because I drew him out of the water" [New Revised Standard Version]. Not only would the meaning remind the people that God had provided for Moses's salvation while he was in the Nile, but also that God had the ability to draw them out of their wandering as well. Therefore, they needed to trust and worship God, not an alternative object of worship.

Another name in the text is Aaron, the priest who is convinced by the people to make a calf for them to worship. His name, meaning "bright" or "shining," could remind the reader that a follower of God needs to be bright and shining in his or her devotion, instead of falling away, as these people did.

The name of Joshua is mentioned only once in the text (32:17), but its meaning is significant: "salvation."[14] This name would remind the people of

12. Way, "God, Names of," *ISBE* 2:1264.

13. Hoffmeier, "Moses," *ISBE* 3:2083.

14. Peloubet, *Peloubet's Bible Dictionary*, 331; Lilley, "Joshua," *NBD*, 612.

the special nature of their God and what he could provide for them. That would lead them to love God more because he provides salvation.

In regards to *nature*, one key animal is featured: the golden calf. The item that enrages God appears in Exod 32:7–8:

> Go down at once! Your people, whom you brought up out of the land of Egypt, have acted perversely; they have been quick to turn aside from the way that I commanded them; they have cast for themselves an image of a calf, and have worshiped it and sacrificed to it, and said, "These are your gods, O Israel, who brought you up out of the land of Egypt!"

Many writers have tried to explain the significance of calves to the Israelites and to God. Knowing what this calf represents is the key to understanding God's anger.

According to Oswalt, "the bull calves . . . are the ultimate symbol of apostasy."[15] The reason that the calf became something people would worship is that the Egyptians had represented their god Amon-Re as a bull. They believed that the bull was the physical manifestation of Amon-Re, so they worshiped it. Similarly, the people were convinced that they were worshiping the visible Lord in the valley below.[16] In Exod 32:4 they said, "These are your gods, O Israel who brought you up out of the land of Egypt." Their sin was not changing from one god to another, but trying to represent their God in a physical form. But that can only be understood by knowing how Israelites, who had grown up in Egypt, understood the significance of the calf.

The *numbers* in Exod 32 that should be understood to promote the idea of love are two and 3,000. Moses was carrying "the two tablets of the covenant in his hands" as he descended the mountain (32:15), which may be significant. Later passages in the Law made it clear that for a person to be executed, there must be two witnesses against them (Deut 17:6). When Moses enforced the death penalty, his two witnesses were the two tablets. Although the Ten Commandments were given in Exod 20, they weren't written until chapter 32, when Moses brought them down from Mount Sinai. Jewish tradition said that one tablet contained the first half of the commandments while the second tablet contained the second half. The people's actions violated a commandment on each of the tablets. On the first tablet was the commandment to have no other gods, along with this clear injunction from Exod 20:4: "You shall not make for yourself an

15. Oswalt, "Golden Calves," 13.

16. Ibid., 19.

idol in the form of anything in heaven above or on the earth beneath or in the waters below." The second tablet contained the command, "You shall not commit adultery" (Ex 20:14), the violation of which the text suggests in verse 6 with "they rose up to revel." Paul also references this event in 1 Cor 10:7, in the context of discussing sexual immorality. Two tablets justify God's punishment of their sin, which does not violate his love.

The other number in the text is 3,000, the number of Israelites who died at the hands of the Levites in one day (32:28). As punishment for this idolatry, Moses had the faithful Levites kill people who were participating in this sin. The number 3,000 is made up of two numbers, 3 and 1000. In the Bible, a thousand is often used as a large, round number. For instance, Psa 50:10 says, "For every wild animal of the forest is mine, the cattle on a thousand hills." The number three reminds us of the nature of God, that he is Father, Son, and Holy Spirit. Perhaps 3,000 deaths signify that because God's nature was being blasphemed, many people had to be punished. The number 3,000 is also in Acts 2:41, the number of people added to the church on the first day the gospel was preached. In contrast to the 3,000 who physically died at the giving of the Law, 3,000 were spiritually saved at the giving of the Holy Spirit on the day of Pentecost. This is a reminder that the way of the Spirit in the New Testament is better than the way of death in the law.[17]

Examining Ambiguities

This passage definitely ascribes severity to God and the saints, which makes it ambiguous in Augustine's description, since God seems to sanction the killing of 3,000 people at the hands of the Levites. Like Augustine, interpreters need a spiritual explanation for this passage to explain it without advocating the slaughter of sinners or denying the historical event. Readers may either wonder "Why did God allow such a horrible thing to happen?" or "Why would such a horrible thing be recorded in Scripture as an example for people to follow?"

17. This point is further developed by Paul in Romans 7:5–6: "While we were living in the flesh, our sinful passions, aroused by the law, were at work in our members to bear fruit for death. But now we are discharged from the law, dead to that which held us captive, so that we are slaves not under the old written code but in the new life of the Spirit." Paul often connects the law with death and the Spirit with life. Although Paul does not appeal to the connection using the number 3,000, I believe Augustine would have (2.16.25).

The answer to that question comes from Augustine in 3.11.17: "Every severity, therefore, and apparent cruelty, either in word or deed, that is ascribed in Holy Scripture to God or His saints, avails to the pulling down of the dominion of lust." To Augustine, lust is the opposite of love, so if a passage can discourage people from lusting, it is in harmony with the overall purpose of Scripture to build up love for God and neighbor. Of course, Exod 32 contains clear examples of lust toward God and neighbor. Lust toward God means using him in ways that he does not intend to be used. That can be seen as the Israelites say that the bulls are their god. Lust towards neighbors would be seen in the "partying" that was going on, when they sat down to eat and drink, and rose up to revel (Exod 32:6). This is not a simple meal, but represents a pagan idolatry ceremony, complete with sexual worship offerings.

Augustine would not remove the historical aspect of the event in order to interpret it spiritually. Instead, he would make the spiritual application now. Many applications can be made to God's people. One is that true followers of God (like the Levites) need to be zealous to serve God and do whatever is asked of them in His service. Another application is that Moses' leadership of some problem people was based on his close relationship with God. He did not first go down and kill them, but prayed on behalf of them. Moses came down from the mountainside and gave the people a chance to change, but he "saw that the people were running wild" (32:24) and made a clear call for people to follow him.

Several applications can be made from this passage without urging Christians to take the sword into their own hands. The analogy of Scripture method reveals other options. For instance, Christians are told to take up "the sword of the Spirit, which is the word of God" (Eph 6:17). Paul advocates using a sword, but not a sharp piece of metal. God's word is "living and active, sharper than any two-edged sword" (Heb 4:12). Even if Exod 32 describes armed attacks against enemies of God, a Christian preacher would encourage Scripture to be the sword used.

Another spiritual lesson from Exod 32 is that Christians should not be idolaters, because God will punish those who are. In 1 Cor 10, Paul compares Christians to the Israelites. Both have identified themselves with a deliverer (Moses or Christ) and have experienced a spiritual food and drink (manna and quail or holy communion). Paul refers to several stories from the Exod time period in 1 Cor 10:7–12. The key application that Paul makes is that the people rose up, thinking that they were safe, but they ended up "falling."[18] In the Christian era, it is also possible for people who think they are standing firm to be near an imminent fall.

Conclusion

In this chapter, I have described Augustine's charity criticism and have interpreted Exod 32 using that method. God's people need to show love for him by forsaking idolatry (the calf) and being zealous to serve him (the sword). It also tells them to avoid lust (reveling), which keeps them from the proper love of neighbor. Such a message encourages more love in Christians who had in the past "turned to God from idols, to serve a living and true God" (1 Thess 1:9).

18. See 1 Cor 10:8.

2

New Testament Narrative Criticism and the Preacher

The Beginning of a Discussion

FRANK DICKEN

Introduction

I SHOULD BEGIN WITH a disclaimer: Chuck Sackett is my father-in-law. I *have* to honor him, if for no other reason than the fact that his daughter (my wife), Jill, will make me. But before he became my father-in-law, he was one of my undergraduate professors. He, along with several other professors, helped me to begin to think carefully about how to interpret the Bible when I was a student preparing to preach. Then I went to seminary, primarily to become a better interpreter of the Bible, particularly the New Testament. Chuck was there, encouraging, challenging, sharing, and teaching. Two weeks after I graduated from seminary, Jill and I moved back to Maryland where we began our first full-time ministry. Though Chuck was living in Illinois, he was "there," especially during some difficult times. When Jill and I moved to Edinburgh, Chuck was "there" too, performing the helpful (but I am sure terribly boring for him) task of reading and proofing my PhD thesis one chapter at a time. And when we moved back to Illinois in 2013, Chuck was there too, unloading the moving van. Yes, I have to honor him, but I also want to, not only for his academic and professional contributions, but for his investment in me personally.

This collection of essays in honor of Chuck focuses on the two foci of his professional career in the church and the academy: homiletics and hermeneutics. In this essay, I want to focus on the latter. Over the last few decades, literature in the field of homiletics has increasingly sought to instruct practitioners in methods of interpretation that are sensitive to the various genres of the Bible. Much, if not all, of this methodological literature operates within the constraints of historical-critical (or grammatical-historical, as it is sometimes called) exegesis. One of my personal scholarly interests is New Testament narrative criticism and I would like to see the insights of New Testament narrative critics applied to the preaching task. I hope that this short essay will be one small step in that direction. I cannot be exhaustive or address every issue. My aim here is much more modest: to compare and contrast the methodology for interpreting the canonical Gospels and Acts expounded by New Testament narrative critics on the one hand and homileticians on the other, with some concluding reflections on how New Testament narrative criticism may be useful to preachers. In short, I hope to challenge and encourage readers of this essay to think in different terms concerning their interpretation of the Gospels and Acts as they prepare for the task of preaching.

Overview of New Testament Narrative Criticism

Several scholarly works have been influential in bringing the literary criticism that came to prominence in the wider academy in the latter half of the twentieth century to bear on New Testament (NT) studies.[1] Though debates concerning the objectives and goals of NT narrative criticism are ongoing, my objective here is to present the basic, general parameters within which such critical readings of Mark, Matthew, Luke-Acts, and John take place.

1. Rhoads and Michie, *Mark as Story*; Culpepper, *Anatomy*. The enduring legacy of these two works are evident not only in the former being issued in a third edition, but by two recent collections of essays that build on their influence: Skinner and Iverson, eds., *Mark as Story: Retrospect and Prospect*; Thatcher and Moore, eds., *Anatomies of Narrative Criticism*. Narrative studies of the gospels of Mark and John have been more prominent than those of Matthew and Luke-Acts. On Matthew, see Kingsbury, *Matthew as Story*. For Luke-Acts see Tannehill, *Narrative Unity of Luke-Acts*, vols. 1 and 2; Talbert, *Reading Luke*; Talbert, *Reading Acts*.

To start, NT narrative critics begin with the assumption that the final form of the Gospels and Acts (or Luke-Acts) each present a unified, consistent story with structural and thematic connections throughout.[2] The text is considered the locus of interpretation, an end in and of itself without regard for the real author or real reader. The following heuristic model provides an overview of the components of both historical-critical and narrative interpretation.[3]

Real →   Implied   Implied   → Real
Author   Author → (Narrator) → (Narratee) → Reader   Reader

The box represents the text of the writing under examination. Historical-critical study concerns itself with the intent and events surrounding the real author. The real author is the historic person who composed the biblical text and the real reader is, in the case of preparing a sermon, the preacher and her or his reading community. Narrative-critical study, on the other hand, concerns itself with what is inside the box. The four "people" inside the box "are internal elements of the discourse itself, with no connection to the real world authors and audiences. They represent, rather, choices that the author makes about how to tell the story, choices that are embedded in, and observable from, the presentation."[4] The implied author is "reconstructed by the reader from the narrative," i.e., the implied author does not *tell*, but instead is understood by repeatedly examining the design of the whole narrative, extracting information about how the story communicates its particular ideology or ideologies (in the case of the Gospels and Acts we might say theologies).[5] We distinguish the real author from the implied author by thinking not in terms of the composition of the text, which is the domain of the real author, but thinking instead in terms of the *form* of the text. The words of Tannehill may be instructive. He writes,

> The implied author is the kind of person who would write this kind of work, which affirms certain values and beliefs and follows certain norms. While there is usually a close connection between

2. See Tannehill, *Narrative Unity*, 1:xiii, 3; Powell, *What Is Narrative Criticism?*, 7–9.

3. Thatcher, "Fourth Gospel," 22. The diagram is adapted from the fuller discussion in Chatman, *Story and Discourse*, 147–151.

4. Thatcher, "Fourth Gospel," 22.

5. Chatman, *Story and Discourse*, 148.

the values and beliefs of the author and of the implied author, the perspectives of the two should not be simply identified. The implied author is likely to be a purified self, more consistent and noble, or perhaps more radical, than the author in external life, and may even be an experiment in being a different sort of person.[6]

The implied reader is also a textual construct, distinguished from the real reader by having its reading anticipated by but limited to the text itself, whereas a real reader's response is unconstrained.[7] Powell describes the implied reader in three ways: 1) it reads the story as it is expected to, 2) knows *only* what a reader of this story is expected to know, and 3) believes *only* what a reader of this story is expected to believe."[8] The narrator and narratee are also textual. They often function like characters in the story, with the narrator being a sort of "voice" in the text and the narratee the hearer of this voice. They are placed in parentheses in the diagram because they are not always present.

"The goal of a narrative critical analysis is to read the text as the implied reader."[9] Since the Gospels and Acts are writings from the first century CE, we should seek to understand these narratives as we would any other narrative text from that period, i.e., with careful attention to the overarching plot of the story, which is the driving concern of Hellenistic narrative.[10] By plot, we mean the story line of the narrative, the beginning, middle, and end. Or, in the words of Aristotle, the elements of plot are order, amplitude (of sufficient length to capture the significance of the topic), unity, and connections between events.[11] We determine the plot of a narrative through repeated readings of the story which will flag up the structural and thematic elements of

6. The words of Tannehill, *Narrative Unity*, 1:7.

7. Powell, *Narrative Criticism*, 19–20. As Powell indicates, the implied reader is not a first-time reader, but rather the reader that knows and assumes everything in the story after multiple readings.

8. Powell, "Narrative Criticism," 24.

9. Powell, *Narrative Criticism*, 20.

10. See, e.g., Moore, *Literary Criticism*, 15. On plot as the most important element of narrative, see Aristotle, *Poetics*, §§6–8. Scholarly consensus sees the Gospels as a specific kind of narrative, biography. See Burridge, *What Are the Gospels?*. There is also a turn toward viewing the Book of Acts as a type of ancient biography, e.g., Adams, *Genre of Acts*; Burridge, "The Genre of Acts—Revisited," 3–28. Burridge, *What Are the Gospels?*, notes the somewhat unclear genre distinctions between biography, historiography, and monographs in ancient Greco-Roman literary culture (237).

11. Aristotle, *Poetics*, §7. On plot analysis and the gospels, see Culpepper, *Anatomy*, 84–86.

the text of the narrative itself. Other narrative devices are subordinate to and supportive of the plot of the story. Exegetical analysis of devices such as characters, settings, point of view, structures and patterns, etc., should reinforce and help shape our understanding of the plot. For our purposes, the plot of the Gospels and Acts may be understood as the evangelists's retellings of the story of Jesus, each with their own distinctive nuances.[12]

The end result of a narrative analysis of the Gospels and Acts (or a selected passage from these narratives, as is likely to be the case for the preacher on Sunday), at minimum will have the following features. First, the analysis will not appeal or refer to anything outside the narrative other than those elements that would be shared by the implied author and implied reader (e.g., language, various cultural items to which the text refers, etc.).[13] Second, conclusions regarding the interpretation of a passage must cohere with the plot of the narrative as a whole. Third, the findings will be restricted to a single gospel, or Luke and Acts together in the case of the third evangelist.[14] Powell summarizes the literary interpretation of the Gospels and Acts in distinction from historical-critical findings as looking in a mirror as opposed to looking through a window. Historical critics view the text as a window through which they hope to glean information about what lies behind the text: either the events that gave rise to the texts or the intentions of the author (the text is referential). Narrative criticism is like looking in a mirror, in which the interaction between the reader and the text gives rise to insights and meaning (the text is poetic).[15]

Various Approaches to Interpreting the Gospels and Acts in Preaching Texts

The Real Author and Real Readers, Not the Implied Reader

We now turn to examples of scholars who have written concerning the interpretation of the Gospels and Acts as narratives in order to contrast their

12. Ibid., 86.

13. For a few helpful examples of such analysis of passages from the second gospel, see Malbon, "Narrative Criticism," 36–47.

14. On limiting the findings to a single writing, see Moore, *Literary Criticism*, 7–8; Rhoads, "Narrative Criticism," 267. On the unity of Luke-Acts, see Spencer, "Narrative of Luke-Acts," 122; Green, "Luke-Acts, or Luke and Acts?"; Keener, *Acts*, 551.

15. Powell, *Narrative Criticism*, 8.

methodologies with that outlined above. What we read in the works of these scholars is careful attention to many of the devices that authors of narratives employ to communicate meaning (scenes, plots, characters, contexts, settings, etc.).[16] However, the hermeneutical methods proposed by scholars of preaching differ with regard to the two key elements discussed above: 1) that the meaning of narratives may be found in the perspective of the implied reader and 2) the centrality of plot in Hellenistic narratives. What follows is not meant to disparage or discredit the works of these scholars in any way. Historical-critical interpretation is and likely will continue to be foundational to the task of expository preaching. Rather, I simply want to note where a few representative scholars differ in their methodologies for interpreting narrative texts.

First, there is a contrast between the end goals of the hermeneutical methods employed by narrative critics and preaching scholars. As we saw above, the narrative critic aims to understand the text as the implied reader does, i.e., knowing everything the implied author does but nothing more than some shared cultural items (language, etc.). On the contrary, the methodologies for interpreting narrative texts espoused by preaching scholars focuses on the real author's intended meaning.[17] For example, Edwards writes, "Your exegetical goal must be 'to recover as accurately as possible the meaning that the original writer intended.'"[18] Also, Greidanus correctly makes the following distinction: "Historical interpretation seeks to understand the text as it was understood by its original audience. Narrative criticism tends to bracket out the historical dimension and concentrate on the self-contained story-world," but follows this up by stating that "historical interpretation is the only objective point of control against subjective and arbitrary interpretations. Moreover, historical interpretation leads to better understanding of a text because it looks for the historical question (the question or perceived need of the original audience) to which

16. For very helpful discussions of interpreting these devices in the context of narratives within a historical-critical framework for the purpose of sermon development see Edwards, *Effective First-Person Biblical Preaching*, chapter four; Arthurs, *Preaching with Variety*, 68–82; Borden and Mathewson, "Big Idea," 274–278.

17. I have chosen the examples of Edwards and Greidanus here because they deal with interpretation of NT narratives rather than a homiletical method that can be applied to any genre.

18. Edwards, *First-Person*, 32. Here Edwards is citing Sunukjian, "Homiletical Theory," 167.

the text is the answer."[19] The interpretive goal of these two leading scholars of preaching is evident: to discover the intentions of the real author.[20] What Edwards and Greidanus propose is interpretation of the gospel narratives that ties the text inextricably to a historical person.[21] The difference with the narrative-critical methodology outlined above is clear—narrative criticism limits its findings to the text itself whereas the hermeneutic employed by Edwards and Greidanus does not.

An exegetical approach that gets closer to the methodology we explored above is that of Joel Green in two essays in the multiauthor volume *Narrative Reading, Narrative Preaching*.[22] Green's concerns are much more significant than employing a hermeneutic sensitive to the contours of Hellenistic narrative; he is seeking to read the gospel narratives within the grand narrative of Scripture and the history of the people of God, which is not only a hermeneutical move, but also a canonical and theological one.[23] With regard to narrative interpretation in particular, Green notes that such an approach must account for the final form of the text as a whole in its socio-cultural contexts and allows for a variety of meanings that are limited by the grammar, syntax, genre, and cultural context of the text itself.[24] Green also notes two realities specific to the genre of the Gospels and Acts that narrative interpreters embrace: 1) the Gospels and Acts are more than the perspectives of the authors and/or communities from which they rose and 2) these writings are not intended to solicit agreement that an event happened or a person said something.[25] However, Green's ultimate concerns do not lie with the implied reader. Instead, for Green, meaning lies with the real reader, specifically contemporary communities of Christians that

---

19. Greidanus, *Modern Preacher*, 299.

20. On the difficulty of determining the real author's meaning in theological construction see Hatina, *New Testament Theology*, 154.

21. Powell, "Narrative Criticism," 26–32 looks at a particular type of narrative criticism—tied to the New Criticism of the mid-twentieth century—that seeks the intentions of the real author. Powell examines the benefits and pitfalls of this approach with his primary criticism being that it amounts to little more than redaction criticism.

22. Green, "(Re-)Turn"; Green, "Reading the Gospels."

23. Green, "(Re-)Turn," 18.

24. Ibid., 25, 27. Green goes on to offer further limits on the meanings of the text, namely the canon and the creeds, but this speaks more to his larger hermeneutical and theological emphases.

25. Green, "Reading," 46–47. Green notes the lack of clear genre distinctions between ancient historiography and ancient biography. See note 10 above.

believe in the authority of Scripture. Accordingly, Green states that correct interpretation of Scripture happens in the regular meeting and discerning of Scripture's meaning in the Christian community.[26] Further, Green writes that narratives invite participation in the narrative on the part of the reader, i.e., the Christian community.[27] With such an approach we have once again gone beyond the bounds of the text itself, not to the historical writer behind the text, but rather the reading community in front of the text.

Again, these two approaches are not to be disparaged or discarded. They are valid methods for discerning the meaning of the Gospels and Acts for the purposes of sermon construction and proclamation in churches. They are not, however, an appropriation of narrative criticism proper.

Plot as a Narrative Device versus Plot as the Primary Concern

The second difference between the literature on preaching narratives and the sketch of narrative criticism I outlined above is the emphasis placed on the plot of the narrative. The methods espoused by homileticians offer various narrative features to which the preacher must give attention: setting, characters and characterization, dialogue, rhetorical structures, plot development, etc.[28] These authors are correct to explain how to analyze these narrative devices, as such analysis is essential for exegesis of narrative texts.

However, subordinating plot to simply another feature of narrative texts rather than understanding it as *the* driving concern does not cohere with the genre of the Gospels and Acts. As noted above, Hellenistic narratives reveal their ideological (theological) perspectives via plot, which is uncovered through repeated encounters with the text that in turn reveal the structural and thematic elements that comprise the plot.[29] Once the preacher grasps the plot of the narrative, then analysis of other narrative features may supplement and inform that understanding.[30] One's under-

26. Green, "(Re-)Turn," 23.

27. Green, "Reading," 47.

28. See e.g., Borden and Mathewson, "Big Idea," 273–278; Greidanus, *Modern Preacher*, 285–295; Arthurs, *Preaching*, 68–82.

29. The concern with plot will likely strike some readers as an attempt to uncover the real author's intended meaning of the narrative. Without a doubt, the plot of the narrative was influenced by the concerns of the real author. However, we must restrict our analysis of the plot to the text of Scripture itself rather than the mind and situation of the author or authors of the texts, which is ultimately historical matters and not textual ones.

30. Characters in particular, through the depiction of their actions and choices, help

standing of the plot may even change based on discoveries regarding other features of the narrative. The preacher, however, must always keep the plot of the narrative as the guiding principle of her or his interpretation. The plot is what the implied reader "hears" and "understands." If plot is both the driving force of Hellenistic narratives and where the implied reader's understanding lies, then the preacher wishing to appropriate narrative criticism in sermon preparation will do well to study carefully the plots of Mark, Matthew, Luke-Acts, and John.

Reflections on the Usefulness of New Testament Narrative Criticism for Preachers

Methodologies abound, and to distinguish one hermeneutical strategy from another is helpful. There are many useful ways that preachers and their listeners can hear the Word of God speaking through Christian Scripture. But, inevitably the preacher will wonder how a new strategy helps with Sunday mornings. Here I offer a few reflections on the usefulness of narrative criticism for the preacher.

Theological Preaching

Determination of how the implied reader understands the plot of the narrative allows the preacher to capture the theological vision of a single narrative, something akin to what certain NT theologies set out to accomplish.[31] However, Christians do not believe in only a single Gospel (a la Marcion). Our narrative interpretations of the Gospels and Acts stand alongside each other and the rest of the Christian canon, including the Hebrew Scriptures. Powell captures this tension in narrative interpretation when he writes,

> Sometimes my unexpected response to Mark's narrative may be due to the fact that I hold to a perspective informed by the whole canon of scripture, not to mention two millennia of theological reflection upon the biblical writings. Ultimately, I believe that a theologically informed, canonical response to Mark's Gospel is preferable to the anticipated response of the Gospel's implied

the reader unravel the plot. On the relation between characters and plot see Aristotle, *Poetics*, §15.1–6, and Tannehill, *Narrative Unity*, 1:3.

31. For two slightly different author-by-author approaches to NT theology see, e.g., Matera, *New Testament Theology*, and Marshall, *New Testament Theology*.

reader. At other times, however, I discover that my response to Mark's narrative diverges from what would be expected of the implied reader because I have been ignorant or because I have been stubborn or selfish—and, then, respect for the narrative's status as scripture does motivate me to conform my response to what would have been expected of me.[32]

This is the tension with which the preacher who appropriates narrative criticism must live. While a narrative interpretation may be an end in and of itself, it is also, in a sense, a preliminary step that deepens our understanding of the theological nature of the entire canon of Scripture.[33]

The Text as the Locus of Meaning

Preachers are called to proclaim the text of sacred Scripture. By bracketing out the intended meaning of the real author, narrative criticism allows meaning to reside in the text of Scripture itself rather than in the minds of mostly unknown authors. This distinction may seem like splitting hairs to some, but it is an important distinction nonetheless. Narrative criticism forces us to focus on the text of Scripture, which is recoverable. Historical-critical/historical-grammatical exegesis seeks the intentions and thoughts of the authors of these texts, a proposition made difficult by several factors (historical, hermeneutical, epistemological, etc.), but not least by the fact that the authors of the canonical Gospels and Acts are unknown.[34] As Christians, we believe that the authors of Scripture were inspired, but it is the text of Scripture that we believe is the Word of God. Powell is once again instructive when he writes that a text-oriented hermeneutic that seeks the perspective of the implied reader may provide believers with an authoritative interpretation that "equals what the biblical book means for people who receive it in a manner expected of them."[35]

---

32. Powell, "Narrative Criticism," 41–42.

33. A helpful approach to preaching Old Testament narratives may be found in Long, *Preaching*, chapter 5. In this chapter, Long espouses many of the concerns I have noted above with regard to interpreting NT narratives, particularly with attention to the theological beliefs of the writers and communities which gave rise to the texts and are evident in the plot and characters of the narratives themselves.

34. The traditional ascriptions of the Gospels and Acts to two apostles, Matthew and John, and two followers of apostles, Mark and Luke, arose in the second century.

35. Powell, "Narrative Criticism," 43.

Conclusion

What has been examined above is a distinguishing between methods for interpreting New Testament narratives; space has only afforded me the opportunity to present a brief sketch. The preacher unacquainted with narrative criticism may follow up with some of the resources cited in the footnotes. I am convinced that narrative criticism offers contemporary preachers a fruitful interpretive strategy. The shift from discerning the intended meaning of the real author (the goal of historical-critical/grammatical-historical exegesis) to understanding the perspective of the implied reader will take practice. Admittedly, it is an adjustment. But the effort is worth it, for in doing so we and our listeners may hear afresh the words of these sacred texts.

3

The Speeches in Acts as a
Rhetoric of Relevance

Neal Windham

RELEVANCE IS RELATIVE. THAT is, what's quite relevant to one person may
appear almost entirely irrelevant to the next. Mothers of infants and tod-
dlers see a healthy stash of diapers as quite relevant, for example, while
middle-aged bachelors could, for the most part, care less. Farmers notice
the weather like hawks searching sparrows, but children wish only to know
if their parents will make them wear a coat to school, and so on. Ultimately,
diapers and coats matter to just about everyone (just ask some of those
bachelors when they're 90), and this fact illustrates a crucial point about
relevance which we'll come to in a moment. But for now, suffice it to say
that the reasons for which diapers and coats matter, the degrees to which
they matter, and the seasons of life during which they matter most vary
widely from one person to the next.

Relevance with Some Size to It

Generally speaking, the more detailed and intricate the subject (say, the
taxonomy of Greek nouns or verbs), the greater the probability of its irrelevance to a wide audience. And, conversely, the greater the size of a subject
(love, beauty, and war come to mind), the more likely its widespread appeal,

at least at the surface level. Nuclear armaments, hurricane economics, and 9–11, for example, have been hot topics for virtually everyone living in North America at some point, but the feeding habits of striped bass, clearly interesting to marine biologists and fishermen on the Chesapeake Bay, are not quite as relevant to most of us, or at least they don't appear to be.[1] In truth, what we are aware of is relevant, but a fraction of all that is relevant throughout the world. That is, just because we don't see the relevance of some concern does not in any way make it less of a concern, particularly for those affected by it directly.

Perhaps the greatest problem with our distorted views of the relevant is that all too often what seems most relevant is only that which we perceive to affect us personally, with little thought to its impact upon our communities, let alone the planet. Moreover, what matters most to us, at least at the conscious level, is profoundly limited due to our finite capacity to take in and really absorb the facts of human experience.

If, on the one hand, we are concerned about global issues like ecology and hunger and war, that is well and good. The relevant really is relevant— to everyone. But if what is *most* relevant to us (whether we admit it or not) is a hunting trip, or a shopping spree, or a golf game, then heaven help us. We have become petty and small. We have trained ourselves not to notice others. We have denied empathy (and thus compassion) a real chance. Even sympathy may be a stretch for us.

What is Relevant?

I want to make a categorical statement about relevance. Simply put, *what is ultimately relevant is always relevant to everyone everywhere, whether they know it or not.* Not that rock concerts and the World Series don't matter. It's just that these things don't rate very high when placed alongside the need for global justice, or the plight of the starving, or, for that matter, the existence of a God who created us and cares about all these things. Lasting relevance is, in the final analysis, always about ultimate things.

Having said this, I must hasten to add that what is most relevant may or may not be something you and I think about a lot. But if our hearts are tuned to what is most relevant—salvation, compassion, truth, injustice, and

1. Major fluctuations in the population of menhaden, one major food source of these fish, are in reality a pretty big thing for people making a living fishing the bay, and thus also for those of us who enjoy eating striped bass.

the like—it is a clear indication that the Holy Spirit is gradually steering us Godward.

Resurrection Relevance

So the question becomes, "What do we who are traveling the Christian path do with personal and popular interest in the things of God? How do we move both ourselves and other people caught in smaller narratives to the one great overarching story of God's consuming love for all creation?" Or, to put it differently, "How do we position ourselves to allow God's Spirit to make this move for and in us? How do we negotiate the turn from transitory irrelevance to ultimate relevance, from games, gimmicks, and gadgets, to God?"

The answers to these questions are as varied as the people offering them. Some call attention to the importance of establishing physical spaces conducive to worship, others to proper forms of liturgy, others to what seems most relevant to contemporary people (ethical business practices, steady relationships, raising good teens, etc.). And who would argue that any of these things is wrongheaded or bad or even off base? Each matters.

With relevance in mind, I notice one thing about the speeches (or sermons) in Acts. Every single one of them targets the resurrected Jesus as Lord of life. And, as we've said, what's ultimately relevant is actually relevant. For Luke, that means resurrection relevance. Listen to the sermons of Peter and Paul: "This prophecy was speaking of Jesus, whom God raised from the dead, and we all are witnesses of this. Now he sits on the throne of highest honor in heaven, at God's right hand. And the Father, as he had promised, gave him the Holy Spirit to pour out upon us, just as you see and hear today" (Acts 2:32–33, ESV). "You rejected this holy, righteous one and instead demanded the release of a murderer. You killed the author of life, but God raised him to life. And we are witnesses of this fact!" (Acts 3:14–15). "When they had fulfilled all the prophecies concerning his death, they took him down from the cross and placed him in a tomb. But God raised him from the dead! And he appeared over a period of many days to those who had gone with him from Galilee to Jerusalem—these are his witnesses to the people of Israel" (Acts 13:29–31). "God overlooked people's former ignorance about these things, but now he commands everyone everywhere to turn away from idols and turn to him. For he has set a day for judging the world with justice by the man he has appointed, and he proved to everyone who this is by raising him from the dead" (Acts 17:30–31).[2]

Weigh the primacy of the resurrection in Luke's mind. He highlights this central Christian teaching in at least six distinct ways. First, the resurrection shows up in at least a dozen major speeches in Acts. Virtually every sermon in the book mentions it explicitly. So the resurrection is statistically relevant. Second, as we saw in several of the verses quoted above, the apostles, and particularly Peter, viewed their primary work as that of witnesses to the resurrected Lord Jesus. Thus the resurrection is also evangelistically relevant. Third, the resurrection was often seen as fulfilling Old Testament promises, especially those related to David. It is thus hermeneutically relevant. Fourth, the resurrection was a scandal both to Greeks (17:32) and Jews (26:8), and in this sense it may be said to be intellectually relevant. Fifth, the resurrection was the principal reason for the imprisonment and trial of Paul. It is in this sense apologetically relevant. And, sixth, Paul consistently portrayed the resurrection as the indispensable grounds for his hope in Jesus. It is therefore, and perhaps most importantly, eternally relevant.

What's actually relevant is what's always relevant. True enough. But I would go even further. In truth, again, *that which is most relevant is that which matters to all people in all places at all times, whether or not they are aware of it.* If I were to tell you that Jesus rose from the dead—physically and bodily—and that because of this we can too, don't you think this news would qualify as more relevant than anything else? Stocks and bonds, new cars, and even better-paying jobs pale in light of resurrection life. Look at the money we're putting into health care and, on the seamy side, the illicit and growing corpse-for-cash trade. People really do want to live forever! But God has a better idea; resurrection transcends, even defies, these worn-out shells. Ultimately, we know in our bones that the afterlife, or whatever you care to call it, matters deeply.

A Rhetoric of Relevance

So how did Peter and Paul convince the interested crowds who flocked to God's miracle that, like this Jesus, they too could live forever in a real body made new?

What follows is a detailed picture of one way to examine a sermon in Acts for clues to improving one's preaching. New Testament scholars are

2. See Acts 1:22; 5:30; 7:56; 10:40; 24:15; 26:8; 28:20.

working closely with ancient forms of rhetoric in an effort to help us understand just how Peter and Paul reached their audiences. While there are different rhetorical techniques at work in the New Testament, and while the speeches of Acts in their present form appear to utilize no one set pattern, we can still detect at least some of the elements of these ancient forms in the many sermons scattered throughout the book.

For example, in Paul's sermon to the Athenian philosophers (Acts 17:22–31), there is an introduction (meant to gain a hearing), a stated goal (to acquaint them with the "unknown god"), a section of proof (where Paul argues his case that the Judeo-Christian God is the one true God), and a concluding summons (which elicits a response to this speech in anticipation of coming judgment). Even Peter, whose audience is very Jewish, does something similar back in Acts 2.[3]

What I am wondering is whether we can use a similar approach today in sharing the resurrection-faith story. Think about it. In Acts 2, the strangeness of tongues, the need for an explanation, and the fact that "God speaks *my* language" all interest and excite the crowd, leaving them with a desire for more. And just what, as a preacher, does Peter do with this desire?

A Theoretical Matrix for Relevant Preaching

Consider these elements of interest in Peter's sermon back in Acts 2. When the disciples began speaking in tongues: (1) *curiosity* was aroused, as the strange sights and sounds appealed to (2) the *imagination,* which thrives on the odd and spectacular. Next, (3) *inquiry* into the mystery of the gift of tongues ("Are not all these men speaking Galileans?" 2:7b) gave way to (4) *exploration,* as the crowd stayed on for Peter's examination of the day's events in light of Old Testament texts. If this pattern is true to the facts of human experience in any age and setting, as indeed it seems to be, then a Christian's resurrection witness should pay attention to these four elements. Each serves as a point of contact or engagement between speaker and audience, between witness and seeker. Each is a God-given faculty of the mind, perfectly natural and healthy. When properly addressed and understood, each invites and often compels interested listeners to turn toward God.

The problem today is that often Christian witness neither invites curiosity nor stirs imagination, neither sparks inquiry nor offers exploration.

---

3. For a more technically precise description, see Witherington, *Acts,* 518.

And the same can be said of much contemporary preaching. Simply put, it is, for whatever reasons, irrelevant.

But Peter's response to the crowd's questions was anything but irrelevant. To the contrary, he engaged the crowd not only with curiosity, imagination, inquiry, and exploration, but also with:

- *Acquaintance* between Peter and his audience (in the introduction to Peter's speech), a "getting to know you" kind of thing (Acts 2:14)

- *Identification* of and even with the principal character of this new movement of God, the resurrected Jesus (part of the goal of this speech, Acts 2:22–23)

- *Connection,* so that the inquirers could see that Jesus makes sense of and is directly connected to their world of understanding and experience (incorporated into the proof section of Peter's speech using sacred texts, Acts 2:24–35)

- *Conviction,* because the miracle cries for a conscience-searing port of entry into the heads and hearts of the crowd (the first part of the summons in this speech, Acts 2:36–37)

- *Call,* because even with a safe port of entry there must be an invitation to navigate the harbor safely all the way home (the second part of the summons in Peter's speech, Acts 2:38–39)[4]

What could happen if we were to take the four elements of interest cited (curiosity, imagination, inquiry, and exploration) and analyze them closely alongside the five "sections" of Peter's speech as we have outlined it here (acquaintance, identification, connection, conviction, and call), creating a theoretical matrix for relevant Christian preaching? I believe that this approach will allow us to examine the speech in such a way that we can see how its many crisp details help us to pinpoint important connections and raise crucial questions with the audience, which in turn will help us to see just how to lead people to a faith encounter with the risen Lord. To see just how this works, first read Acts 2:14–40. Then, carefully read and think through important connections with the crowd as they are depicted below

---

4. Granted, these five categories do not align perfectly with the rhetorical scheme Witherington presents in his commentary on Acts noted above. However, neither does Peter's scheme square perfectly with ancient rhetorical practice in general. He seems to be taking at least some liberties. For example, as Witherington notes, the *narratio* section is missing in Peter's speech (Ibid).

in Matrix 1. Please note that in general you should read the matrix first from left to right and then from top to bottom, always in that order. While this is not a tightly wound, hyper-linear presentation, it nevertheless does follow a very general order of presentation as I have set it up here.

Matrix 1: Christian Witness and Spiritual Transformation at Pentecost

Peter engages the crowd	A. Curiosity	B. Imagination	C. Inquiry	D. Exploration
1. Peter *Acquaints* . . .	Who are you, preacher? Do you know me? (See Acts 2:14, "Fellow Jews," and 22, "Fellow Israelites.").	Peter knows Joel's fantastic images matter to his audience, and thus quotes Joel (Acts 2:17–21).	Do Pentecost events have anything to do with the religious texts and personal experiences of Peter's audience as these show up in Joel?	Peter and his audience begin to ponder Joel's words deeply in light of the events of this day.
2. Peter *Identifies* . . .	What does Jesus of Nazareth have to do with the events of this day? (Acts 2:22).	Jesus performed deeds of power, wonders, and signs similar to those of Joel 2:28ff.	How can Peter's audience know that Jesus is somehow tied to their God?	Multiple identifications of Jesus provide clues to his identity: accredited by God, Lord, Christ, etc.

Peter engages the crowd	A. Curiosity	B. Imagination	C. Inquiry	D. Exploration
3. Peter Connects . . .	What do these tongues and this Jesus have to do with me?	Jesus of Nazareth is the one about whom David prophesied (Acts 2:31). Fulfilled prophecy grabs the Jewish imagination.	What does David's prophecy mean as applied to Jesus? And what does all of this mean for me?	Unlike David, but on the basis of David's words, Jesus is the resurrected Lord. Peter ties into a prevailing Jewish and Pharisaic "orthodoxy" here.[5]
4. Peter Convicts . . .	Am I in any way tied to Jesus' death and resurrection?	The crowd begins rethinking the days of Jesus' Passion, their part in it, and its ultimate meaning.	Did I in some way contribute to Jesus' earthly demise?	Yes, the crowd did indeed participate in Jesus' death according to Peter (Acts 2:36).
5. Peter Calls . . .	What are the implications of Jesus' death (and my part in it), resurrection, and Lordship for me?	A period of complete religious disorientation sends the imagination in many competing directions.	What on earth can we possibly do about all this (2:37)?	Believe. Repent (all of you). Be baptized (each one of you). Receive forgiveness and the very Spirit who inaugurated the events of this day.

5. Though with a twist. As Tom Wright has noted, while the Pharisees believed in a general resurrection at the end of history, Jesus' resurrection in the "middle" of history

Putting the Matrix to Work in Your Preaching

As you have probably noticed, at each intersection within the matrix I have made observations or raised questions designed to help you think hard about how human faculties like curiosity and imagination couple with rhetorical elements like acquaintance and identification in order to open up a meaningful dialog between Peter and his audience, as well as you and yours.

In order to illustrate how the matrix works, I want to examine the first row, acquaintance, point for point. Notice first that at 1.A, where curiosity meets acquaintance, Peter and the crowd are just getting to know each other. By calling his audience "Fellow Jews," Peter ties himself to the crowd in a very concrete way. These curious listeners needed and wanted a credible, empathetic interpreter of the day's events, one upon whom they could surely rely for accurate truth telling. By identifying himself as one of the crowd (a fellow Jew), Peter begins to establish this key connection early in the address. Placement and timing are crucial.

Similarly, as faithful witnesses we must recognize that those to whom we speak in Jesus' name will want to know who we are, how well we know their stories, and how we've actually walked with them in a variety of ways (religiously, vocationally, or racially, for example) early in our acquaintance. At the very least, they will need some assurance that we have attempted to understand them and take their viewpoints seriously. Otherwise, they may well write us off from the very start. Acquaintance at the personal level matters deeply in relevant Christian witness. It should be established early in any faith encounter.

Now look at the connection in 1.B, where Peter appeals to the imagination with Joel's fantastic images of things like the sun darkened and the moon turned to blood. He knows that the Old Testament is a particularly sensory-laden canon, from its intimate, fleshy descriptions of the creation of Eve, to the near-sacrifice of Isaac, to the compelling visuals of the prophets, and beyond. Thus Peter uses the familiar and carefully selected vision of Joel to address the novel tongues of Pentecost with deep appeal to the imagination, a divinely given faculty of the mind useful in evangelistic encounters. In other words, he utilizes a known and respected spiritual reference point (Joel's prophecy) in his explanation of an unknown and perhaps disturbing spiritual phenomenon (the tongues of Pentecost).

---

was to them an anomaly. See Wright, *Surprised by Hope*, 45; Wright, *New Testament and the People of God*, 200, 328.

Taking our cue from Peter, today we might well call attention to the unbridled volunteerism of young Christian servants who are making their way around the world, clothing the naked, visiting the sick, preaching the good news to the poor, and feeding the hungry—all actions and images taken directly out of Isaiah and Matthew 25. These caring actions, by way of anecdote and documentation, "echo" texts familiar to many modern and postmodern people who are at least somewhat familiar with the Bible, cementing the deep meaning of Christian faith in action in the hearts of seekers everywhere, helping them to see that God is yet hard at work in today's world, summoning them to more. Can we not use such a known reference point (say, Isa 61 or Matt 25 or James 2) to call attention to a new spiritual phenomenon? Those spiritual phenomena are, for example, the unbridled Christian volunteerism in New Orleans in the Katrina era, or the many who have become involved in ministry to victims of sex trafficking? And is it not possible that this kind of acquaintance will gain a hearing among seekers for what we have to say about the gospel itself? At this stage, we're simply trying to engage the imagination of a seeker for God.

As a third example of how to use the matrix, think about 1.C (acquaintance/inquiry). Here we ask, "Do Pentecost events have anything to do with the religious texts and personal experiences of Peter's audience?" In other words, "Why are you (Peter) applying Joel 2:28–32 to *this* situation?" The question is a very good one insofar as people are deeply concerned about how the church uses the Bible, that is, about how and why preachers pick the texts they do for their sermons. Some have been victims of manipulative (and perhaps even fraudulent) "evangelists" who are interested only in bilking their savings accounts. Credibility demands a clear explanation as to how a given text fits a real-life situation. Peter's role is one of demonstrating that the events of Pentecost fulfill the prophecies of Joel and the Psalms of David in concrete ways.

All of which raises the very serious question, "How do our lives and congregations 'fulfill' ancient texts, demonstrating beyond dispute that contemporary disciples are actually living what they profess to believe?" Remember, we're at the level of acquaintance/inquiry, which means people are looking at us to see whether there is in reality anything to what we're talking about, or whether our Christian "speak" is anything more than a smoke screen.

Finally, in 1.D, where acquaintance meets exploration, it seems we have finally come to the place where Peter can now actually begin to explore and ponder events of the day of Pentecost in light of Joel's prophecy (Joel 2:28–32). That text was first applied to a theophany, a painful awareness of the need for God's abiding presence in the midst of profound darkness and deep suffering.

Peter's approach here is heavy for a get-acquainted party, but seekers aren't looking for fluff. This intersection in the matrix reminds me of a personal faith encounter I had some years ago. While speaking with an elderly woman who'd once been a Christian but had since given up her faith upon the loss of her husband and then her son, I was searching deeply for just the right words to share with her. This was a door-to-door encounter, and I didn't have a lot of time to think through what I'd say. (Perhaps I was not trusting God to provide the right words as I should have!) On further reflection, later in the day, I concluded that I should have explored with her the deep suffering of Christ as it is depicted in Philippians 2:6–8 (a text I think she would have known), in an effort to help her see that Christ knows the very kind of pain she was feeling. I also wish I'd had the courage to say something like, "You once had a loving husband, son, and heavenly Father. I know your husband and son are gone now, and I can only imagine how deep your pain runs, but just whom do you have left? You had no control over the loss of either husband or son, but you do have a say in whether you try to stick it out with God. Please don't give up on him now." Honestly, I don't know what direction the conversation might have taken at that point, but at least this question and observation, based on the matrix, might have forced her to think in fresh, new terms about life, faith, and eternity. And that is precisely what the exploration column is all about—pondering the deep meaning of questions and texts as these apply to real-life situations like hers.

One thing I do know: this woman, once a faithful believer, had lost hope, and she was searching for answers. It would not be easy to help her find them, either. This one-time faith encounter in a town a thousand miles from my home simply would not do. I wish I'd had time to look deeply into her life and faith with multiple encounters, perhaps using a tool like this matrix, in order to help her cross the faith threshold.

Customizing

Notice how the matrix can be useful in formulating the right questions, approaches, examples, and summons in our witness and preaching today.

This will require work. I recommend that you select a seeker, or an audience within the church, whom you know pretty well, and ask yourself just how this matrix may, point for point, help you to connect with and summon your friend(s) to faith in Jesus. I have not commented on every square within the matrix precisely because you will have to customize (and because this essay is already getting out of hand!). As you do so, try to determine just where your audience is. Are they just getting acquainted with you and your story, or are they actually trying to identify who Jesus is? Are they ready to consider how they are connected to Jesus, or are they in some way convicted by the truth of his story? After you've determined where they are in the conversation, go to the right row (acquaintance, identification, etc.), and think through its interface with curiosity, imagination, inquiry, and exploration as these play out for your specific audience.

The plain truth is that effective evangelistic preaching is generally not a one-time encounter with someone who knows she's searching for eternal life. The days of the successful "crusade" are pretty much over. Rather, it is generally a carefully connected series of both strategic and spontaneous encounters where faith is shared, lived, and explored in close personal relationships which lead to conversion. Constant attention to where seekers are "located" in the matrix should prove fruitful in addressing them as they are and where they are.

But What Do I Say to People Who Do Not Believe in God?

Matrix 1 is built around one sermon addressed to one monotheistic audience in one setting at one time. As such, it will not do for everyone. Based upon a sermon that Paul preached while in Athens to a group of Greek philosophers (Acts 17:22–31), the following matrix is quite different from its predecessor. Where Peter's sermon was preached to Jews who believed in Yahweh (the LORD God of the Old Testament), Paul's was preached to pantheists and polytheists, people who believed in many gods. While the rhetorical structure of the two sermons is in some ways similar, the lines of reasoning, religious texts cited, and appeals to faith are quite different.

Note the following salient background features: (1) Paul was preaching to Greeks, not Jews, to people who did not know or attempt to follow the Jewish Bible of Paul's day, what we Christians call the Old Testament. Rather, they followed various pagan sources in their religious practices. (2)

Paul's audience honored many gods, but it was in particular an "unknown god" (or unknown "gods") who, according to Diogenes Laertes (*Lives of the Philosophers* 1.110), had abated a plague in Athens some time earlier, to which Paul called attention.[6] 1.110, had abated a plague in Athens some time earlier, to which Paul called attention.59 (3) Paul used this "unknown god" to help the Athenians identify the true God of Judeo-Christian faith, thus introducing them to the gospel. (4) Still, Paul was identified as one who scattered seeds of religious confusion with his preaching. In fact, the crowd may have thought he was introducing not one but two new gods, Jesus and Anastasis (a Greek word meaning "resurrection;" Acts 17:18). (5) Paul quoted a Greek source (Aratus, 2.D.) in his defense of the Christian God. While this author does not constitute scripture for Paul, he is nevertheless quite willing to let truth speak for itself where he sees it. So he is using a text familiar to his audience in order to identify and connect with the best of their religious thought.[7]

Matrix 2: Encountering the Philosophers on Mars Hill

Paul engages the Areopagus	A. Curiosity	B. Imagination	C. Inquiry	D. Exploration
1. Paul *Acquaints* . . .	Who are you, Paul? Do you know us?	Paul appeals to a certain "unknown god."	What is this new teaching you are offering us? (You seem to be a "seed-scatterer").	Paul: "You are religious people with a religious nature. Let's unpack that."

---

6. Parsons, *Acts*, 246. As represented by Diogenes Laertes, *Lives of the Philosophers* 1.112. See Bruce, *Acts*, 384.

7. Aratus, "Phaenomena," 206.

Paul engages the Areopagus	A. Curiosity	B. Imagination	C. Inquiry	D. Exploration
2. Paul *Identifies* . . .	What does the unknown god have to do with Paul's deity?	The unknown god in Greek mythology . . . just who is this god? (Consult a commentary for help with this.)	How is the unknown god tied to Greek religion and life as Paul's audience knows it?	Examine your own poetry: "In him we live and move and have our being," and "We are his offspring." What are these writers saying?
3. Paul *Connects* . . .	Paul, am I in some way tied to this deity you speak of?	Paul speaks of temples, life's origin, nations, boundaries, etc. Who is behind Paul's argument?	But how can it be that the unknown god is actually connected to me personally, as you seem to be suggesting?	You are seeking him, and he is not far from any one of you, says Paul. Let's think hard about what that means.
4. Paul *Convicts* . . .	Does your unknown god expect anything from me?	Ponder the resurrection of the "one whom God appointed" and its implications for people created by the unknown god.	How was I supposed to know that the unknown god made me and raises the dead?	You weren't. God overlooked your ignorance, but now the situation has changed.

Paul engages the Areopagus	A. Curiosity	B. Imagination	C. Inquiry	D. Exploration
5. Paul Summons . . .	What are the personal and immediate demands of this unknown god and the resurrection of which you speak, Paul?	Religious confusion over the nature of the unknown god's demands, as well as the very notion of resurrection	Can we talk some more?	Yes, we can. Belief in the one who comes to judge the world and bodily resurrection (not the Greek notion of a soul liberated from its body) is a good place to continue this conversation.

Do you see how different the first and second matrices are? As we have noted, the point is that we need *relevant* homiletical and evangelistic preachers. These matrices may be customized to fit specific audiences and situations. The second matrix fits the needs of people who believe in a plurality of gods, as well as people possessed of the so-called "secular" mind-set.

Still More Relevance for Today

In case all of this seems too much of a stretch, a third (and final) matrix suggests even more ways (very direct, contemporary ways) in which Christian witness and life transformation might come together in an evangelistic sermon. Its questions and suggestions are based upon our earlier matrices, but it is broader in its approach. It may prove useful in at least three ways: (1) to establish just where people are in their faith journey, (2) to help identify crucial elements we should include in contemporary evangelistic preaching, and (3) to give direction to present and future encounters with seekers on a customized basis. I suggest that you try to see which question in this matrix best fits a specific real-life situation, and then work forward through the rest of the matrix with your audience. Meet them where they are and take them where they need to go.

Matrix 3: Contemporary Witness & Personal Spiritual Transformation

Relevant Witness Today	A. Curiosity	B. Imagination	C. Inquiry	D. Exploration
1. *Acquainting*	Who are you, Christian? Do you really know me?	Explain to me why true worship makes people feel so good & keeps them coming back to church.	How does the Bible figure into this Christian equation?	Consider a few basic texts on the love of God for his creation.
2. *Identifying*	What does Jesus have to do with transformed lives? Why not some other religious figure?	Locate and study texts that show how Jesus relates to & transforms lives.	How is Jesus related to my current religious experience, and, for that matter, to God?	Identify Christ in the contemporary world: Jesus vs. the gods of our times.

Relevant Witness Today	A. Curiosity	B. Imagination	C. Inquiry	D. Exploration
3. *Connecting*	What does Jesus have to do with me?	Meditate on: (1) the grandeur and holiness of God and (2) the broken-ness and sin of people, of me.	Why did Jesus, who did not have to leave glory or suffer our brokenness, have to join us, join me, on the earth?	Explore the meaning and significance of Jesus' coming—death (atone-ment), burial (Jesus really died, just as we do), and resurrection (hope)—as these are depicted in the Bible.
4. *Convicting*	Can I possibly be connected to Jesus?	Think hard about the way my life relates to God's holiness.	Am I in any way respon-sible for Jesus' death?	Ponder and pray about our sinful human condition.
5. *Calling*	What will it mean for me to live with and for Jesus?	Meditate on life both with and without Christ's presence and God's love.	Is there a concrete way for me to become a follower of Jesus?	Believe. Repent. Be baptized. Experience forgiveness. Receive the Spirit.

The observations and questions in this third matrix aren't necessarily based upon a single encounter with a preacher or another Christian witness. Rather, I have broadened the basic ideas of the first and second matrices (particularly the first) in order to help you connect with modern seekers from a broad cross section of society. As with the others, you must customize this matrix in order for it to work for you. You will select the

Scripture texts you'll use. You will become conversant with the "religious" texts of your audience, say, *The Gospel of Thomas* or Meister Eckhardt or the Koran or Dan Brown's *The DaVinci Code*. You will guide the seeker, helping them to meditate on the images offered in Column 2, the imagination column, based upon your awareness of the seeker's life setting and interests.

Yes, this is hard work. No, it can't be done in a single sitting. All I am doing is providing you with a matrix that can help customize evangelistic preaching in an effort to make the message of Christ relevant.

Conclusion

I hope these three matrices may invite thoughtful participation between you and your audience, especially those who question the relevance of Christian faith to their lives, families, spiritual yearnings, and occupations. The approach is very direct in its trajectory of acquaintance, identification, connection, conviction, and call. There are no distractions here and no gimmicks. While these matrices are very sensitive to those seeking God, they nevertheless make the point that, short of genuine belief in the once-dead, now-resurrected Christ, there is no salvation. In fact, precisely because of their sensitivity to the real condition of profound human need in multiple life settings are they potentially effective. In the final analysis, the sermons of both Peter and Paul demonstrate for their respective audiences that God is here today and he cares deeply about people everywhere.

Not surprisingly, this marked sense of divine presence is precisely what seekers demand in their entire worship experiences today. For if there is no sense that God is present in Christian worship—whether highly liturgical or free and spontaneous, cathedral or house church—and there is no credible, caring summons to belief in the saving Jesus as resurrected Lord of life in the sermon, then interest will eventually be quashed, and the crowd will go home disillusioned. There will be no trace of lasting relevance, no sense of anything ultimate, nothing to hold on to. What will be left is irrelevance—the very thing my dear colleague and friend, Dr. Chuck Sackett, has ceaselessly worked to eliminate from pulpits all over the Midwest, and indeed the world, during his distinguished career as Professor of Homiletics at Lincoln Christian University.

4

Transformational Preaching

J. Kent Edwards

Mark Twain was right when he observed that "teaching is not telling. If it were telling, we'd all be so smart we couldn't stand ourselves."[1] True teaching is not just telling. We want educators who do more than simply upload data into their students. We want teachers that will help their students go beyond information to implication and then to transformation. We want them to help us go beyond "what?" to "so what?" and reach "now what?"

Teachers that go beyond telling to transformation empower their students to carry the concepts learned in the classroom into real-life situations. They ensure that the information being transferred makes a substantive difference in the lives of their students and the community in which they live.

Biblical communicators should share a similar passion. As communicators of God's truth, our goal should be not only to transfer data, but to apply its concepts so that the lives of our listeners are transformed. We need to go beyond "what?" to "so what?" and reach "now what?"

Preachers as Educators

Many evangelical preachers overemphasize the teaching of biblical data. The structure of their sermons seems to assume that if their listeners grasp

1. Rosebrough and Leverett, "Faith and Transformational Teaching," 47.

the language, grammar, and historical and theological context of a pericope of Scripture then the preacher's task is complete. The assumption appears to be that knowledge of the biblical text will automatically lead to moral transformation, even though the Bible indicates that this is not true.

In Luke 4, Satan came to Jesus in the wilderness and tempted him to sin by accurately quoting Bible passages. Clearly Satan's knowledge of Scripture had not resulted in godly character. In John 5:35, Jesus condemns the Pharisees because "You study the Scriptures diligently because you think that in them you have eternal life. These are the very Scriptures that testify about me, yet you refuse to come to me to have life" (John 5:35, NIV). The Pharisees' problem was not a lack of biblical knowledge, but their refusal to allow the truth of Scripture to transform them.

Jesus comments in Luke 11:28 that the "Blessed . . . are those who hear the word of God and obey it" and in John 14:15 that "If you love me keep my commandments" underscore the importance of transformational preaching. It is also the reason that he concluded his sermon on the mount in Matthew with the following statement:

> Everyone who hears these words of mine and does not put them into practice is like a foolish man who built his house on sand. The rain came down, the streams rose, and the winds blew and beat against that house, and it fell with a great crash.[2]

Preachers do not and cannot fulfill their calling by simply communicating biblical information. Learning is more than telling. Preachers need to go beyond "what?" to "so what?" and reach "now what?" The spiritual consequences of not doing so are devastating, as Richard and Shera Melick point out:

> Many people sit under Bible studies each week at church . . . they know many facts about Christianity, but many show no evidence that their thinking has changed. Their lives seem no different. . . . Teachers may teach the Bible to the same learners year after year and nothing happens. We hear and see but do not act. Education is not as much about knowing as it is about learning. Learning is measured by life change. Teaching is quantifiable. Learning is qualifiable. God's primary concern is not the amount of material we have been taught but rather, in our progress toward becoming more like Christ.[3]

2. Matt 7:26–27.

3. Melick and Melick, *Teaching That Transforms*, 258.

Preachers Are Educators

While it is true that preachers are more than educators, it is also true that they are not less than educators. The demands of biblical preaching require that we take up the challenge of good educators and go beyond "what?" to "so what?" and ultimately reach "now what?"

The question that every biblical preacher must answer is: how can my preaching extend beyond the informational to the transformational? Educational theory can help us answer this question because "although adult education theory often has secular presuppositions . . . the Christian educator can glean helpful teaching principles that will enhance adult learning."[4] As Mark Noll stated so well,

> If God made all humans in his image, if the ability to learn about the external world is a gift given by God to all those made in his image, if Scripture teaches that believers in God are also susceptible to error, and if scripture testifies repeatedly that all people have a significant capacity for genuine insight on some aspects of human affairs—then Bible believers should be the first to expect genuine intellectual insights from the entire human community.[5]

One prominent adult education theorist that can help preachers reach the "now what?" stage in their sermons is Jack Mezirow.

Transformational Learning Theory

Jack Mezirow is the adult educational theorist who pioneered the work on Transformational Learning Theory.[6] Like biblical preachers, Mezirow is concerned about ideas. He realizes that people's ideas determine the courses of their lives. While many ideas are transferred to us from our parents or society, Mezirow encourages adults to identify and examine their core beliefs for themselves. This reexamination is critical for Mezirow because he believes that "uncritically assimilated presuppositions may distort our ways of knowing . . . our ways of believing . . . our ways of feeling . . . that control

---

4. Ibid., 3.

5. Noll, "Bible, Baptists," 97.

6. Mezirow, *Fostering Critical Reflection*; Mezirow, *Transformative Dimensions of Adult Learning*; Mezirow, *Learning as Transformation*; Mezirow and Taylor, *Transformative Learning in Practice*.

adult feelings and behavior."[7] Since a person's behavior springs from their beliefs, Mezirow is convinced that the purpose of adult education is to:

> help adult learners become more critically reflective, participate more fully and freely in rational discourse and action, and advance developmentally by moving toward meaning perspectives that are more inclusive, discriminating, permeable and integrative of experience.[8]

Respected evangelical homiletician Haddon Robinson shares Mezirow's high view of the importance of ideas. Robinson agrees that people's beliefs shape their actions when he states:

> Through ideas we make sense out of the parts of our experience. All ideas, of course, are not equally valid; we have good ideas and bad ideas. Bad ideas offer explanations of experience that do not reflect reality. They read into life what is not there. Often we embrace invalid ideas because they have not been clearly stated and therefore cannot be evaluated. In our culture, influenced as it is by mass media, we are bombarded by ridiculous concepts that are deliberately left vague so we will act without thinking.[9]

Meanwhile, Mezirow states that the goal of his Transformative Learning Theory is to

> transform our taken-for-granted frames of reference (meaning perspectives, habits of mind, mind-sets) to make them more inclusive, discriminating, open, emotionally capable of change, and reflective so that they may generate beliefs and opinions that will prove more true or justified to guide action.[10]

Robinson echoes this language when he asserts that the task of biblical preachers is to "confront, convict, convert, and comfort men and women through the proclamation of biblical concepts . . . [because] people shape their lives and settle their destinies in response to ideas."[11]

It appears that Transformative Learning theorists and biblical preachers have much in common when it comes to valuing people's ideas and appreciating how behavior can be transformed through careful corporate

7. Mezirow, *Transformative Dimensions of Adult Learning*, 5

8. Ibid., 224–225

9. Robinson, *Biblical Preaching*, 20.

10. Mezirow, *Learning as Transformation*, 8.

11. Robinson, *Biblical Preaching*, 20.

reexamining of those ideas. It may also be that there is much that they can learn from each other.

How Transformation Happens

While Mezirow asserts that transformation "may be epochal, a sudden, dramatic, reorienting insight, or incremental, involving a progressive series of transformations in related points of view that culminate in a transformation in habit of mind,"[12] he suggests that transformation typically follows some variation of the following phases:

1. A disorienting dilemma
2. Self-examination with feelings of fear, anger, guilt, or shame
3. A critical assessment of assumptions
4. Recognition that one's discontent and the process of transformation are shared
5. Exploration of options for new roles, relationships, and actions
6. Planning a course of action
7. Acquiring knowledge and skills for implementing one's plans
8. Provisional trying of new roles
9. Building competence and self-confidence in new roles and relationships
10. A reintegration into one's life on the basis of conditions dictated by one's new perspective[13]

While a thorough examination of each of these phases is beyond the scope of this essay, the phases of Transformation Learning Theory can help biblical preachers transform lives with the ideas of Scripture. While Mezirow's transformational phases are homiletically applicable to all biblical genres, they fit particularly well with biblical narratives.

12. Mezirow, *Learning as Transformation*, 21.
13. Ibid., 22.

Understanding Biblical Narratives

Biblical narratives are stories in which inspired narrators communicate theological ideas wrapped in the lives of historical characters. Narratives are composed of a series of scenes that are combined into a single plot. Adele Berlin likens the scenes of Hebrew narratives to

> the frames from which films are made. Each one exists separately, and they are combined in a certain order to make the greater narrative, but the individual frame has no life of its own outside of the film as a whole.[14]

The arrangement of scenes reveals the plot of a story. Far from being random, scenes are arranged by the narrator in order to advance the plot.[15] The factor used to determine the arrangement of scenes is conflict. Longman points out that "plot is thrust forward by conflict. The conflict generates interest in its resolution. The beginning of a story, with its introduction of conflict, thus pushes us through the middle toward the end, when conflict is resolved."[16] Leyland Ryken agrees that

> Stories are always built around plot conflicts. These conflicts progress toward some type of resolution, and when the resolution occurs, closure comes quickly . . . [a basic] rule for reading stories, is to identify *the exact nature of the plot conflicts in a story, noting how they develop and are resolved.*[17]

A helpful tool that can aid in the recognition of narrative plot structure is the monomythic cycle. Reg Grant identifies the monomythic cycle as "the archetypal pattern true of all literature" and uses the book of Ruth to demonstrate that Ruth's "plot structure is comic/monomythic. As such, it manifests four literary structural elements as the plot moves from tragedy through anti-romance, and then through comedy to romance."[18]

14. Berlin, *Poetics and Interpretation*, 125.

15. Edwards, *Effective First-Person Biblical Preaching*, 41.

16. Longman, *Literary Approaches*, 93.

17. Ryken, *How to Read the Bible*, 41.

18. Grant, "Literary Structure," 424.

Monomythic Cycle

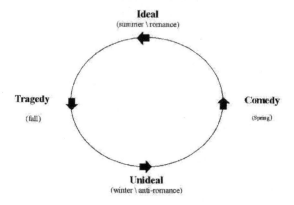

In the "romance," "ideal," or "summer" stage of narrative plot, the reader is briefly treated to an ideal experience, or life as the characters in the story (as well as the reader) would like it to be. In the "tragedy," or "fall" segment of the narrative, the equilibrium of events is upset by a negative situation or inciting event. The tragic portion of a narrative describes a downward fall from bliss to misery. This negative series of events culminates in the literary element of "anti-romance," "unideal," or "winter." In its pure form, anti-romance is "an existence devoid of joy."[19] The "comedy," or "spring" phase of a narrative describes a surprising reversal of events that transforms a tragic story back into a literary "ideal," or "summer" phase.

Biblical Narratives and Transformational Preaching

The literary structure of biblical narratives provides preachers with a wonderful opportunity to utilize the phases of Mezirow's Transformational Learning Theory to help their listeners integrate biblical ideas into their lives. The exegetical portion of sermon preparation consists of using the monomythic cycle to determine the beginning and end of the biblical narrative and locating the main idea of the story. The idea of the story is found where the plot takes an unexpected twist from "winter" to "spring." Once the exegesis is done, the homiletics is surprisingly simple.

19. Ibid., 431.

Step One—Understand the people

I recommend that the preacher begins by taking a blank sheet of paper and creating three columns. At the top of the first column, write the protagonist's name; at the top of the second column the preacher should write their own name; and at the top of the third column write the word "listeners."[20]

Since the idea of a biblical narrative is typically revealed in the actions of the protagonist, the preacher should begin by listing in the first column *everything that can be known* about the protagonist. Questions such as profession, age, temperament, education, family background, etc., should be asked. The goal here is to get to know the protagonist as well as the biblical text allows.

In the second column the preacher should outline the *similarities that exist between themselves and the protagonist*. In what ways are their lives similar to that of the protagonist? Traits such as hopes, talents, fears and pressures and weaknesses should be explored. The goal is for preachers to see themselves reflected in the life and struggles of the protagonist.

In the third column the preacher repeats the process, but does so *on behalf of their listeners*. How does the protagonist relate to the people who will listen to the sermon? In what ways is the protagonist similar to them? The goal here is to be able to establish a genuine connection between the audience and the biblical character.

Since this first step is critical for the eventual success of the sermon, I strongly recommend that preachers utilize the illuminating resources of the Holy Spirit as outlined in *Deep Preaching*.[21] God often provides profound insight into the biblical text in response to significant prayer and meditation.

When the first step is completed, the preacher can begin outlining the narrative sermon. For narrative portions of Scripture, I recommend following the monomythic cycle and withholding the big idea until the climax of the sermon. Rather than preaching points, preachers should follow the scenes as presented in the biblical text.[22] Each scene should first be explained, and then parallels should be drawn between what is happening

20. A new sheet of similarly columned paper will be needed for each scene of the biblical narrative.

21. Edwards, *Deep Preaching*.

22. While this is true for shorter narratives, extended stories may require that scenes be dealt with in clusters rather than individually.

in the scene and what the preacher and the listeners experience in their own lives.[23]

[When the strategy of moving through the scenes of a story by alternating perspectives between the historical and the present is done with insight, the listeners become completely immersed in the biblical story. Listeners begin to see the biblical story as their story and the opportunity for transformational learning is enhanced.]

Step Two—A disorienting dilemma

Perhaps the most important element of narrative preaching is to clearly identify the conflict of the story. We could refer to the problem that creates a narrative's conflict as the "disorienting dilemma." Preachers need to begin their narrative sermons by clearly identifying the protagonist's conflict. Once again, I recommend using a fresh three-column piece of paper (as in step one) and identifying why the situation was so difficult for the protagonist, and repeating the question for the preacher and listener. In what ways is the problem faced by the protagonist shared by the preacher and listener? How is their issue, temptation, or struggle similar to what we face in our lives? The goal of this exercise is to link the struggles of the protagonist with those of the preacher and listeners. I desire transference to occur so that the protagonist's struggles are viewed as a common problem by the preacher and listeners.

Mezirow views the disorienting dilemma as a critical component of transformational learning, because people often require a significant crisis before they are willing to reexamine the underlying ideas that created their dilemma. What makes for good narrative preaching also facilitates transformational learning.

Step Three—Self-examination with feelings of fear, anger, guilt, or shame

What Mezirow is looking for in this stage is the engagement of people's emotions. He wants people not only to understand a problem, but also to feel the weight of it. This is an important step in the transformation process because raw logic seldom changes behavior. Take driving habits as an

---

23. The three-column worksheet described above will prove helpful here.

example. Most drivers know that speeding is dangerous, yet many people speed when they drive. What can cause us to change our driving habits, and stay under the speed limit? Probably not a list of accurate and emotion-free statistics. On the contrary, when a person's reckless speeding causes a terrible accident—and they see the blood, pain, and anguish that their speeding has caused others and themselves—and when that feeling is so strong that they are overwhelmed by a tidal wave of emotion (feelings of fear, anger, guilt, or shame) then it is far more likely that a permanent shift in driving habits will occur. A disorienting dilemma that is painful enough to create strong emotions creates an environment where affective learning can occur, and is a necessary condition for transformational learning.

As preachers begin their narrative sermons with an emotional crisis based in the text and then continue through the story, weaving in and out of its scenes, helping the listeners personally identify with the protagonist's struggles, they are setting the stage for transformational learning. As biblical communicators we need the crisis faced by the protagonist not only to be cognitively understood but also emotionally connected to the lives of our listeners. Sermons that don't grip hearts will not change lives.

Step Four—A critical assessment of assumptions

Mezirow's emphasis on the importance of examining the ideas that underlie behavior is critical for effective preaching. It is not enough for biblical communicators to understand the language, culture, context, and geography of a story. They also have to exegete narrative passages psychologically.

Preachers need to ask and answer the question: Why did the biblical character make their decision? This is an important exegetical question because while animals may act out of pure instinct, people always act for a reason. Every decision we make is an expression of the ideas we hold, even if those ideas are held unconsciously. For this reason, the preacher needs to ask and answer questions such as: Why did David choose to cover up his sin with Bathsheba? Why did the Virgin Mary agree to carry Jesus to term? Why did Cain murder Abel?

Since the biblical narrators often prefer to imply truth rather than state it baldly, the answers to these questions may not be obvious in the biblical text. But the careful exegete, under the guidance of the Holy Spirit, can discern the ideas or assumptions that led the biblical character (and the engaged listener) to make the decisions they did.

Having asked this "why" question exegetically, the preacher needs to take another three-column sheet of paper and ask why they have made similar choices as the protagonist. In the third column they need to ask why their listeners have made the same choices.

The task of the transformational preacher is to help their listeners raise to the level of consciousness the ideas that led them to follow in the footsteps of the protagonist. If preachers don't have a clear understanding of why they are making the life choices they do and don't help their listeners do the same, then transformational learning will not occur. It is only when our ideas are exposed that we can examine and reevaluate the concepts that control our behavior.

Step Five—Recognition that one's discontent and the process of transformation are shared

As the preacher continues scene by scene through the biblical narrative, each scene will increase the tension of the disorienting dilemma. Slowly and inexorably the ramifications of the protagonist's initial decision and the idea that spawned it will be acted out in the story. Positively or negatively, the seed that was planted in the first scene will root and grow until the story ends. Stories don't discuss truth, they display it.

Following Mezirow's lead, transformational preachers will not be satisfied with noting that the biblical protagonist may have made a mistake. Nor will they be content with showing how other people fall short of biblical standards. On the contrary, since "there is no one righteous, not even one," (Rom 3:10) preachers who want to be transformational will emphasize the universality of the human condition. Rather than succumbing to Phariseeism, they will demonstrate how all people in all places and in all ages share the idea that caused the protagonist's conflict. The objective here is for listeners to recognize that the conflict in the biblical narrative is not someone else's problem, it is the audience's problem.

Step Six—Exploration of options for new roles, relationships, and actions

The application of this step is delayed until the winter of the monomythic cycle. It is at the bottom of the circle, when the story takes an unexpected twist towards spring and summer (comedy), or ends in winter (tragedy). The reason for the delay is twofold.

First, "winter" is where the emotional power of the story is strongest. As previously noted, emotion is a powerful tool of the transformational process. People are unlikely to seriously consider abandoning their old ideas for new ones unless they "feel" a strong need to do so.

Second, winter is also where the idea of the biblical story is fully revealed. It is here, in the twist towards summer, where we clearly see the benefit of godly ideas and actions. It is also here, in tragic stories that end in winter, where the tragic results of sinful ideas and actions are made clear.

Once the underlying idea is fully revealed, the preacher can hold it up before their listeners and examine it to see if it was true. If it was a wrong (sinful) idea that led the protagonist down a path of disobedience and destruction, then the falsehood of that idea needs to be laid bare. If, however, it was a good (holy) idea that propelled the protagonist towards godliness, then the preacher can identify and champion the idea.

When our listeners see the consequences of good and bad ideas in the context of the biblical narrative, they will be more likely to explore options for new roles, relationships, and actions. Here we can show and tell people why it is urgent for them to exchange unbiblical ideas for those that will allow them to fully flourish.

A Step Further

Mezirow outlines five additional steps in the transformational learning process. These include

- Planning a course of action
- Acquiring knowledge and skills for implementing one's plan
- Provisional trying of new roles
- Building competence and self-confidence in new roles and relationships
- A reintegration into one's life on the basis of conditions dictated by one's new perspective[24]

While it will be helpful for preachers to urge listeners to plan a new course of action, and even to give some examples of what that might look like, it is impossible for a speaker in a public setting to outline a customized

---

24. Mezirow, *Learning as Transformation*, 21.

plan of action for every listener. Planning a course of action, and the subsequent tasks outlined by Mezirow, are better accomplished in a sermon-based small group than a public forum.

More intimate contexts can foster greater vulnerability and accountability than larger formal gatherings. Such settings can allow people to collectively share their success and failures in living out the biblical idea. For these reasons, sermon-based small groups could be highly effective in implementing Mezirow's additional transformational steps.

What Really Matters?

Many of those who listen to our sermons have Bibles; some have numerous copies in a variety of translations. Others boast of also having powerful Bible software on their computers, tablets, and phones. It is easier to access the content of God's word today than ever before in history.

What people need from preachers is not simply to be told the content of the Bibles they already own. Being reminded of biblical content is profitable, but God's people need help to go beyond the "what?" to the "so what?" and to ultimately reach the "now what?" They need preachers who will use everything at their disposal to help them be transformed into the image of Christ with the power of God's word.

5

A General Topic as Part of Biblical Preaching's Hermeneutical Methodology

Eddy Sanders

Introduction

A VARIETY OF METHODOLOGIES exist to develop biblical sermons from a single-theme approach. Every few years a new but slightly varied one appears.[1] These methodologies offer a straightforward process that assists the preacher in her or his exegesis, interpretation, and application of a biblical text. Yet, most of these methodologies omit an element that might aid the preacher. That element is a general topic added to the single-theme methodology. A general topic is distinguished from but related to the central, unifying theme derived from the exegetical process.[2]

This chapter will argue for the inclusion of a general topic in interpretive methodologies for biblical preaching. First, the chapter explores biblical preaching and the single-theme approach. Here Haddon Robinson has laid the groundwork that many have followed. Second, the distinction between a general topic and the central, unifying theme is made. Third,

1. For a recent example, see Akin, Curtis, and Rummage, *Engaging Exposition*.

2. By central, unifying theme the chapter aligns with the definition in Robinson, *Biblical Preaching*, 36: "Terminology may vary—central idea, proposition, theme, thesis statement, main thought—but the concept is the same: an effective speech 'centers on one specific thing, a central idea.'"

the chapter will explore issues related to the inclusion of a general topic as part of a methodology for biblical preaching. Finally, an examination of a sermon that exhibits a general topic that is distinguished from the central, unifying theme concludes the chapter.

Biblical Preaching and the Single-Theme Approach

Haddon Robinson is *the* leading proponent of an interpretive methodology for preaching that centers upon a single theme derived from the biblical text in the last thirty-five years. Robinson writes, "Expository preaching is the communication of a biblical concept. That affirms the obvious. A sermon should be a bullet, not a buckshot. Ideally each sermon is the explanation, interpretation, or application of a single dominant idea supported by other ideas."[3] Robinson's single-theme approach laid the foundational methodology that many interpreters and preachers continue to embrace.[4] Keith Willhite begins his article in *The Big Idea of Biblical Preaching* noting Robinson's contribution: "At least since Haddon Robinson's *Biblical Preaching* was published in 1980, many expository preachers and homileticians have advanced the claim that developing a single sermon idea, proposition, or thesis is the best way to preach an expository message."[5] Although they use different terminology, the concept remains the same in *Effective Bible Teaching* by Wilhoit and Ryken. "To teach a passage effectively, a teacher must be able to communicate a sense of its unity. Educational research has shown that before people can grasp specific details, they need a general framework to which they can relate the specific pieces of data."[6] Similarly, John Stott encourages interpreters and preachers to embrace the single-theme approach. He suggests that in sermon preparation "we should be

---

3. Robinson, *Biblical Preaching*, 35.

4. For examples of those who disagree with Robinson's single-theme approach, see Buttrick, *Homiletic*. Richard Eslinger summarizes Buttrick's methodology in the following conversation: "Buttrick then turns to the gathered preachers and says, 'Now we did not invent this hermeneutic of distillation. . . .[We] distilled out some topic that sounds an awful lot like a sermon title, and that is what we will now preach on Sunday.'" (*Web of Preaching*, 152). Reid states that single-theme "approaches tend to operate with a 'hermeneutic of distillation' that seeks to tease a summarizing 'Big Idea' or a rational conceptualization of the meaning from the text" ("Exploring Preaching's Voices," 144). Reid cites Mathewson's *Preaching Old Testament Narrative* as a recent example.

5. Willhite, *Big Idea*, 13.

6. Wilhoit and Ryken, eds., *Effective Bible Teaching*, 59.

looking for our text's dominant thought . . . every text has an overriding thrust."[7] According to these authors, emphasis upon the text's single theme and its development in the sermon are key to biblical preaching and its methodologies.

Explanation and adaptation of the single-theme approach remains common in biblical preaching circles. In a recent paper, C. J. H. Venter has nuanced the single-theme approach in the following manner:

> The theme is determined from the *telos* of the Holy Spirit, with a specific sermon text from a specific part of Scripture. The theme of an expository sermon does not come externally like a strait-jacket to the text, but summarises the kerygma of the text in the language of today. This implies that the theme should not get bogged down in the process of exegesis, but should cross the bridge and be formulated in terms of today, as the "homiletical big idea" in the sermon.[8]

This definition brings two issues to the forefront related to Robinson's single theme approach. First, the definition is built on the assumption that a theme is essential to biblical preaching when Venter writes, "The theme is determined . . . with a specific sermon text from a specific part of Scripture." Second, the methodology for preaching may, on occasion, require adaptation. Note Venter's language related to the *telos* and the Spirit's role, which is unique to him.

Utilization of the single theme approach remains common in recent preaching textbooks as well.[9] The first example is Donald Sunukjian's methodology as offered in *Invitation to Biblical Preaching*.[10] Sunukjian's methodology is divided into two components. Part One is "Look at What God is Saying . . . ." Part Two is "Look at What God is Saying . . . *to Us*."[11] Part One focuses upon interpretation while Part Two includes both interpretation and delivery. Sunukjian's methodology in Part One builds to "Form[ing] the Take-Home Truth." The "Take-Home Truth" is "the essential core of what the author is saying. It's the idea that dominates all other ideas—it's

---

7. Stott, *Between Two Worlds*, 224.

8. Venter, "Expository Preaching."

9. For the purposes of this chapter, the discussion of methodology and the single-theme approach will focus upon the hermeneutical aspect of biblical preaching.

10. Sunukjian, *Invitation to Biblical Preaching*.

11. Ibid., 19–84; 87–303.

the 'Big Idea,' the central truth the author is trying to get across."[12] Sunukji-an's argument from this point forward in the book explores the elements necessary to effectively communicate that "take-home truth." The elements include hermeneutical issues such as asking the right questions[13] and selecting effective answers.[14] Both of these sections focus on developing the single theme from the text. Throughout Sunukjian's methodology, the focus of the single theme permeates the discussion. He urges the reader to "make the take-home truth simple and crisp so that the listener can easily grasp it."[15] After this, Sunukjian focuses on effective delivery of the sermon with emphasis upon the take-home truth.

The second example of the single-theme approach is Sidney Greidanus' methodology as offered in *The Modern Preacher and the Ancient Text*.[16] Unlike other hermeneutical methodologies, Greidanus' methodology is not a stepped process. Instead, Greidanus walks the reader through a variety of issues related to single-theme preaching.[17] Greidanus' approach to biblical preaching urges the reader to utilize a single theme for the sermon. He writes, "The theme of the sermon is a summary statement of the unifying thought of the *sermon*. Like the text's theme, the sermon's theme is not a subject or a topic but an assertion; it seeks to articulate the message of the sermon in one short sentence."[18] Greidanus' statement raises an important point. Greidanus, like Sunukjian and Venter, lead the interpreter to a theme *sentence*.[19] This theme sentence encapsulates the message of the text for the

12. Ibid., 66.

13. Ibid., 87–127.

14. Ibid., 128–135.

15. Ibid., 137.

16. Greidanus, *Modern Preacher*.

17. Ibid., 1–23. The first issue for Greidanus is preaching as expository preaching. Second, Greidanus discusses the historical-critical method and its impact upon biblical preaching. Chapters 3–5 discuss interpretation from literary, historical, and theological perspectives. Fourth, Greidanus' approach to biblical preaching includes essential elements of expository preaching: textual-thematic preaching, the form of the sermon, and the relevance of the sermon. The final four chapters, nearly half of the book's contents, focus upon generic issues that (should) affect the sermon. See Ibid., 24–341.

18. Ibid., 136.

19. Space does not permit a discussion of other texts such as Richard, *Preparing Expository Sermons*, and Mathewson, *Preaching Old Testament Narrative*, that have similar approaches to single-theme biblical preaching. For a recent hermeneutics text that leads the interpreter to the theme sentence, see Duvall and Hays, *Grasping God's Word*.

sermon. It is the "sermon in a nutshell."[20] Yet, the question remains, how is the single theme different from a general topic?

Distinguishing the Topic from a Single Theme

The single-theme approach arrives at its theme, written as a sentence, as a result of the interpretive methodology. The leading proponent, as mentioned above, is Haddon Robinson.

> An idea consists of only two essential elements: a *subject* and a *complement*. Both are necessary. When we talk about the subject of an idea, we mean the complete, definite answer to the question, 'What am I talking about?' . . . The subject of a sermon idea can never be only one word. . . . Single words such as *discipleship*, *witnessing*, *worship*, *grief*, or *love* may masquerade as subjects, but they are too vague to be viable.[21]

The importance of the theme sentence in biblical preaching cannot be overemphasized. There is a step to which Robinson alludes that could precede the single-theme sentence formulation and enhance the interpretive methodology and, in turn, aid interpreters.

That step is to identify a general topic that is distinguished from but related to the single theme of the text. Kent Edwards writes in *Deep Preaching*, "The *topic* of a passage is like the flesh of a peach. Like the flesh of a peach, the topic of a passage is most accessible to us. The topic of a passage is the *broad subject* that the original author was addressing."[22] Edwards' statement alerts interpreters and preachers to an issue omitted in single-theme methodologies.

Edwards is not the only one to note a general topic in the interpretive process. Carter, Duvall, and Hays offer the following statement in *Preaching God's Word*. They write, "You may want to write down some of your initial impressions about the major themes or emphases of the book as a whole.

---

20. See Richard, *Preparing Expository Sermons*, who writes, "[The central proposition of the Text] is *always* in the form of a full grammatical sentence. If it is less than a sentence, it is not a proposition, by definition" (67).

21. Robinson, *Biblical Preaching*, 41.

22. Edwards, *Deep Preaching*, 69. Edwards' *Deep Preaching* leans more in the direction of a homiletical philosophy than single-theme methodology.

Whatever conclusions you come to after looking more closely at your passage will need to be consistent with what you see in your overview."[23]

Deep Preaching and *Preaching God's Word* stand alone in their *brief* discussions of a general topic as part of a single-theme methodology. Yet, authors in biblical studies include a general topic as part of their interpretation. David J. A. Clines, in his monumental book *The Theme of the Pentateuch*, offers a hermeneutical argument for a general topic.

> To discern the "theme" of a work is a *more perceptive* undertaking than to discover its "subject." Statements both of theme and of subject may be answers to the question, What is the work *about*? But to identify its subject is merely to classify, while to discover its theme is to see "the attitude, the opinion, the insight *about* the subject that is revealed through a particular handling of it," that is, to *understand* the work more deeply than merely knowing its "subject" requires.[24]

Clines, in this paragraph and throughout the book, defines and explores theme in relation to the Pentateuch. He distinguishes between "theme" and "subject." It is important to notice that Clines develops the theme *from* the subject. In Clines' foundational biblical studies text, the general topic is distinguished from but related to the central, unifying theme of the text.

In his *The Thematic Unity of the Book of the Twelve*, Jason LeCureux argues that a general topic is crucial to interpreting Old Testament prophetic literature.[25] In his discussion of the thematic unity of Isaiah, the broad subject is a short phrase or word rather than a developed and focused theme:

> I agree with prophetic scholars that there can be multiple themes that exist in a prophetic work, however, I am also inclined to support the possibility of one dominant, or "controlling" theme, which asserts influence over the others. This controlling theme provides a means of understanding and relating to the other themes that appear in a prophetic work. It is also worth noting that from these references, scholars often use one word to communicate a theme (Zion, turning and returning) or idea (Davidic dynasty, kingship of God). In actuality, it is probably best to understand

---

23. Carter, Duvall, and Hays, *Preaching God's Word*, 53. Though these authors use the term "overview" in comparison to Edwards's "broad subject" or this essay's "general topic," it is the same concept.

24. Clines, *Theme of the Pentateuch*, 20.

25. LeCureux, *Thematic Unity*.

these "one word" themes as abbreviated references to a longer thematic statement.[26]

LeCureux distinguishes a topic, the broad subject of the passage identified with one word, from the text's single theme in his statement that scholars "understand these 'one word' themes as abbreviated references to a longer thematic statement."[27]

An objection at this point is that Clines' (and LeCureux's) "theme" is Robinson's "subject," and Clines' "subject" is Robinson's "complement." Therefore, a general topic is unnecessary in single-theme methodologies because Clines and Robinson suggest the same approach with different labels.

A speech communication text addresses the potential objection observed in Clines' argument. *A Speaker's Guidebook* by Dan O'Hair, Rob Stewart, and Hannah Rubenstein, urges speakers to identify a broad topic first. They write: "The first task in preparing any speech is to select a topic and purpose for speaking."[28] Implicit in their statement is the need for a broad subject.[29] This is what Clines' argument does for the Pentateuch and Robinson's argument for homiletical method omits.

O'Hair, Stewart, and Rubenstein argue that the student of public speaking should move from a general topic to a narrowed topic to a thesis statement. "Once you have narrowed your topic . . . your next step is to formulate a thesis statement."[30] Thus, a three-step process.

It is unlikely that O'Hair, Stewart, and Rubenstein are versed in the process of hermeneutics, sermon preparation, and single-theme methodologies as discussed in this chapter. Yet, their field of speech communication's relation to biblical preaching is precisely why the hermeneutical process and preaching methodologies might benefit from a generalized topic.[31] If a general topic is important to and the first step for public speaking, it could benefit preachers utilizing single-theme methodologies. It would give them

26. Ibid., 31.

27. Ibid.

28. O'Hair, Stewart, and Rubenstein, *Speaker's Guidebook*, 96.

29. The book encompasses most types of speeches, including sermons. See Ibid., 329–417.

30. O'Hair, Stewart, and Rubenstien, *Speaker's Guidebook*, 109.

31. Haddon Robinson references speech communication authors and sources in his discussion of the "big idea" approach to biblical preaching. See Robinson's argument in the section "The Importance of a Single Idea" in his *Biblical Preaching*, 35–39.

a guiding framework early on in interpretation that arises from the initial overview of the text.

A comparison of O'Hair, Stewart, and Rubensteins' argument to Haddon Robinson's methodology in *Biblical Preaching* reveals the following:

	General Topic	Narrowed Topic or Subject	Thesis or Complement
Haddon Robinson in *Biblical Preaching*[32]	None	How will God bring judgment on Judah?	God will use the wicked Babylonians to punish His people.
O'Hair, Stewart, and Rubenstein in *A Speaker's Guidebook*[33]	Blogs	Three benefits of keeping a blog	Maintaining a blog provides the opportunity to practice writing, a means of networking with others who share similar interests, and the chance to develop basic website management skills.

The chart demonstrates that Robinson's methodology overlaps with O'Hair, Stewart, and Rubenstein's at two of the three points.[34] Robinson's methodology omits the general topic.

Biblical preaching emphasizes the importance of the thesis sentence, as discussed above.[35] However, several biblical scholars call attention to the importance of a theme or broad subject. This broad subject or general topic is largely ignored in single-theme methodologies. Why is a broad subject crucial in biblical studies, yet largely ignored in single-theme

32. Robinson, *Biblical Preaching*, 45.

33. O'Hair, Stewart, and Rubenstein, *Speaker's Guidebook*, 122.

34. Robinson overlaps with other speech communication texts as well. See Fraleigh and Tuman, *Speak Up*, 174–184.

35. Greidanus writes, "The theme is a summary statement of the unifying thought of the text" (*Modern Preacher*, 134).

methodologies? The broad subject is an important component of the text and its interpretation.

A second objection arises. The sheer size of the texts Clines and LeCureux discuss is much larger than most textual units for sermons. Clines focuses his argument on the entire Pentateuch, while LeCureux's unit is first Isaiah and then the Book of the Twelve. Kent Edwards addresses this objection. He writes, "If you were to slice open a biblical passage you would see four major elements: a natural unit, a topic, a subject, and a complement."[36] The size of the text is irrelevant for Edwards. Each textual unit has a general topic.

The question that the essay addresses expands: Why do authors in biblical studies include a general topic, a standard speech communication text urges speakers to begin with a general topic, and yet single-theme methodologies ignore the general topic? Single-theme methodologies that include a general topic would assist interpreters and preachers. A general topic could serve as the frame that the proposition, that crucially important sentence, paints with clarity. If a sermon should be a bullet rather than buckshot, the general topic is the barrel that gets that bullet moving in a general direction.

Adding the Topical Component to Biblical Preaching

The inclusion of a general topic for single-theme methodologies has support in recent work in hermeneutics and homiletics. First, Andreas J. Köstenberger and Richard D. Patterson, in their massive volume *Invitation to Biblical Interpretation*, mention the importance of a topic. They write, "By starting with the big picture or broadest category . . . our method embodies the principles of interpreting the parts (words) in light of the whole."[37] Their "broadest category" is the general topic, as discussed in this chapter.

Köstenberger and Patterson's discussion of the narrative genre will serve as an example of the importance of a general topic. In their discussion of Luke 8, they write, "Luke weaves these stories together not only to show Jesus' authority, but the extension of his authority to his disciples to proclaim the

36. Edwards has defined the topic of the passage as "the *broad subject* that the original author was addressing" (*Deep Preaching*, 68–69).

37. Köstenberger and Patterson, *Invitation to Biblical Interpretation*, 25. They go on to argue, "Thus we don't start with analyzing the details of the biblical text; we start with the whole" (26).

kingdom of God."[38] The broad subject in their first step to this point could be "The extension of Jesus' authority" or simply, "Jesus' authority."[39]

Second, C. J. H. Venter also alludes to the necessity of ascertaining a general topic when reading the text: "The preacher should undertake the first reading and re-reading of the text in his or her mother-tongue. . . . This is also the moment when the 'big idea' of the preaching portion is established. . . . A refined formulation takes place at the end of the process of exegesis."[40] At this point in Venter's interpretive process, the preacher does not have a final formulated statement and subject/complement. Instead, he or she may only have a broad subject based on textual observations. In other words, the preacher may only have written and concluded, "The extension of Jesus' authority," to use Köstenberger and Patterson's example. Venter's suggestion employs the general topic concept, although that phrase is not used *per se*.

A third inclusion of a general topic in a methodology for preaching comes from Greg Heisler in a 2008 article in *Preaching* entitled "The Expository Method." In this helpful overview of an expository, single-theme methodology, Heisler offers a series of steps for preparing and delivering an expository message. In the third step, "Survey the Context of Your Text," he writes, "Expository preaching takes very seriously the context in which a textual unit is found. This is the 'fly-over' view, or the panoramic picture. . . . In context [of Philippians 4] the overall framework of 4:10–23 is not superhuman ability, but rather spiritual satisfaction—contentment—regardless of circumstances."[41] Heisler's discussion possesses a general topic, although he doesn't label it as such.

Köstenberger and Patterson, Venter, and Heisler mention a general topic prior to their final and formal single-theme sentence, though the label is different. Their early and initial general topics are not their final single-theme sentences. Rather, they are short phrases that serve as an early frame

---

38. Ibid., 755.

39. What is observed here in Köstenberger and Patterson's interpretive methodology is their process that works from the "first dimension of the hermeneutical triad, history and the various literary facets of Scripture in descending order from the macro- to the micro-level—(from canon to genre to language), we have come to our final destination: theology" (ibid., 693). Köstenberger and Patterson's methodology focuses the general topic or broad subject with precision at each hermeneutical step until they arrive at a thesis statement. See their examples on pages 743–756.

40. Venter, "Expository Preaching."

41. Heisler "Expository Method," 23–24.

of reference for the text. As their discussions reveal, this early-identified general topic served as a guiding frame of reference from which their single-theme sentence eventually emerged. It appears that a general topic aided and assisted their interpretive processes, though they never used that label.

An Example of Adding the Topical Component to a Sermon

The inclusion of a general topic is a missing but necessary component in biblical preaching's methodology. Yet, the general topic is found in biblical studies and speech communication texts. Since biblical preaching includes resources and skills from those disciplines, a general topic as part of the interpreter's study that is distinct from but related to the central, unifying theme would benefit biblical preaching. As an example of how a general topic benefits a sermon, this chapter will conclude with an exploration of a sermon that utilizes a general topic. That sermon is Chuck Sackett's "Somebody Cares," published in *The Journal of the Evangelical Homiletics Society*.[42]

"Somebody Cares" begins with an introduction that includes five paragraphs that move the audience to the sermon's theme. In this introductory section, Sackett discusses his transition from the classroom to the pastorate and acknowledges his audience as teachers of preachers. The introduction focuses largely upon the reality that "talk is cheap."[43] Sackett's introductory image of "cheap talk" contrasts with his text, 1 Corinthians 12, where talk alone will not suffice in the Christian community: "[Verse 25] is buried in all this language about what it means to be a part of the body of Christ."[44] He references two translations that alert the audience to "concern" and "care." This is his general topic.

Sackett moves from the text to the central, unifying theme of the sermon. He writes, "The church is the church when everybody knows somebody cares."[45] As the title of the sermon makes clear and the central, unifying theme explicates, the sermon is about caring. Specifically, caring for one another within a church community. Sackett's general topic has

---

42. Sackett, "Somebody Cares," 117–125.

43. Ibid., 117–118. The audience could have been alerted to the general topic early with a statement such as "People know talk is cheap. They want to know if anybody cares."

44. Ibid., 118.

45. Ibid.

transitioned from a word (care or concern) to a sentence (The church is the church when everybody knows somebody cares.).

After his explanation of the central, unifying theme, Sackett moves the audience through related themes in Scripture. Christian caring is authentic concern and genuine worry as Matthew 6 and Philippians 2 suggest. The message of the text is striking as Sackett writes "just think about the context, the larger context of First Corinthians. . . . This is a body of people who are self-promoting, self-indulging, they are sinful, they are selfish, they are segregated, they are everything that you can imagine, and they are saints."[46] In this five-paragraph explanation, Sackett uses the general topic of care and concern in four of the paragraphs. "If we can't do it to each other, if we can't demonstrate it on each other, if we can't practice taking *care* of each other, how will we ever be able to take it out into the streets and demonstrate it to people who aren't like us?"[47]

Sackett then reminds the audience "And so we care for one another," a return to the general topic. He continues the next section with a reminder of the general topic: "When we care for one another in the context of the body of Christ . . . ."[48] He then tells a personal story of a student who visited him and was struggling. Though he does not use the words "care" or "concern" here, it is evident as he recounts the situation: "And I said, 'I've got to ask you a personal question. You don't have to answer it if you don't want to, but I've got to ask it. How did you make it?'"[49] Sackett embodies care, the sermon's general topic, in his first-person story. Though he did not phrase it in this manner in the sermon, Sackett cared enough to ask.

Sackett then addresses the audience directly. He recounts the story of an audience member who he saw demonstrate care with positive repercussions. From there, Sackett writes, "So what does it look like to care for one another?"[50] The final section of the sermon concludes with another story of care in the midst of difficulty: "And those we are teaching to preach will preach with clarity and with power when they have learned how to care for one another."[51] The sermon closes with an adaptation of the central, unifying theme "that when The Somebody cares they have experienced the

46. Ibid.,119.

47. Ibid.,120.

48. Ibid.,121.

49. Ibid.,122.

50. Ibid.,124.

51. Ibid.,125.

fact that somebody cares."[52] The sermon concludes with a fresh spin on the general topic and emphasis on the single theme of the sermon.

Sackett's sermon is an example of one that utilizes the general topic throughout the message. The general topic remains the focus of the message and the single-theme sentence focuses that general topic.

A few observations are in order based on Sackett's sermon in relation to the general topic. First, Sackett never allows the general topic of the sermon out of the audience's mind. The longest gap is four paragraphs. And as noted above, although the four paragraphs fail to mention the general topic, "care," Sackett embodies care and concern as he recounts how he asked a student personal questions.

Second, of the twenty-five paragraphs in the sermon, fourteen have some form or synonym of the general topic "care." Well over half of the paragraphs remind the audience or offer theological explanation of Christian care and concern.[53]

Third, although "caring" is not mentioned in the first five paragraphs and in the personal story found in paragraphs fifteen through eighteen, it is implicit. It might have been helpful to include a statement that alerts the listener to "caring" in the second paragraph when he writes, "Talk is cheap— really, really cheap [but as we'll see today, Christians who care demonstrate incredible value to those around them.]. "Might" is appropriate because Sackett attempted to engage the audience. "If talk is cheap," the audience might have asked, "then what counts?" "Genuine Christian concern" is the inferred answer.[54]

Conclusions

First, recent single-theme authors get relatively close to including a general topic as part of their process. Those authors do not include that step *per se*, but the concept of a general topic is evident as essential in their interpretation of a sermon text. Second, including a general topic could enhance single-theme methodologies. As observed in "Somebody Cares," sermons may only state the single-theme sentence once or twice, while the general

---

52. Ibid.

53. A helpful resource in relation to writing for the ear is Jacks, *Just Say the Word!*

54. Sackett is using an engaging introduction to begin the sermon. "Engage the listeners' interest, using as many paragraphs as necessary to create a need for, or curiosity about, the message" (Sunujkian, *Invitation to Biblical Preaching*, 192).

topic is mentioned numerous times. The interpreter who has taken a moment to define the broad category in the sermon would be more inclined to communicate that one topic from his or her text rather than shift to other peripheral topics. When the interpreter communicates that one topic from his or her text, the audience hears a biblical sermon that remains focused on the emphasis of the text.

6

The Perpetrator and the Preacher
It's Sunday, Can You Come Out and Play?

JONATHAN HUGHES

THE CEO AND THE board sat around the conference table discussing the quarterly sales figures, which had dropped sharply in the last six months. One optimistic board member suddenly got an idea and piped in among the others in the cheeriest voice she could muster, "What if we don't change anything at all . . . and something magical happens?"

If you are a human, you've been in that room, but the room was in your home, church, seminary, or locker room. No one says these words out loud, but it is what the group has decided by either their actions, or, more likely, their inaction. It is the reality staring every preacher in the eye on that weekly trip to the front of the congregation to speak on behalf of God from the Scriptures.

As a preacher who revels in biblical studies, reads theology, and thinks about ministry every day, when I'm on vacation and visit a foreign church to hear a preacher speak, he or she has their work cut out for them. I know what I believe. I know what I think. I'm set in my ways. I know what I want to do after the service is over and what restaurant I want to visit. I'm suspicious and skeptical, and I do not care (yet) about the text or topic for the morning homily. This is the attitude of a guy who has devoted his life to preaching. So how does everyone else feel about the topic at the beginning of the sermon? If the congregation listens, is there hope for life change as a result of the next twenty-five minutes, or even a year's worth of sermons? The preacher has to work hard to get the attention of the listener and then must overcome at least two obstacles in the hearer: neurological frames and postmodern suspicion.

Neurological Frames

The first obstacle is the neurological frame of the hearer. Alan Deutschman, in his article "Change or Die," illuminates the fact that even when positive healthy changes are the most important factor in the future of one's life, people still don't change.[1] The article reveals "a relatively small percentage of the population consumes the vast majority of the health-care budget for diseases that are very well known and by and large behavioral."[2] These behavioral issues are too much eating, drinking, or smoking, and not enough exercise. Around 600,000 people have bypasses each year in the US and 1.3 million patients will have angioplasties at a cost of around $30 billion, but will not experience long-lasting improvements in health.[3] Another statistic in Deutschman's article reveals "if you look at people after coronary-artery bypass grafting two years later, 90% of them have not changed their lifestyle."[4] This statistic is a staggering account of human resistance to change.

We mistakenly think that if we simply "give the facts" people will change their lives, which unfortunately plays off of one of the chief myths of the Enlightenment. George Lakoff, professor of cognitive science and linguistics, says the first myth of the Enlightenment is that the truth will set us free. "If we just tell people the facts, since people are basically rational beings, they'll all reach the right conclusions."[5] The reality is, people don't think in facts, but in frames. Lakoff writes:

> Neuroscience tells us that each of the concepts we have—the long-term concepts that structure how we think—is instantiated in the synapses of our brains. Concepts are not things that can be changed just by someone telling us a fact. We may be presented

1. Deutschman, "Change or Die," http://www.fastcompany.com/52717/change-or-die, accessed August 29, 2014.

2. Ibid.

3. Ibid.

4. Ibid.

5. Lakoff, *Don't Think of an Elephant!*, 16

with facts, but for us to make sense of them, they have to fit what is already in the synapses of the brain. Otherwise facts go in and then they go right back out. They are not heard, or they are not accepted as facts, or they mystify us: Why would anyone have said that? Then we label the fact as irrational, crazy or stupid.[6]

This is why political or religious discussions often end with one or both parties walking away saying, "Those people are ridiculous," or some other statement revealing that the exchange wasn't an evaluation of ideas but rather individuals bouncing their facts against the frame of their interlocutor.

How many sermons have been preached with the preacher armed with exegetical insight, historical theology, and theological sophistication, hammering on his point only to find that the message has not accomplished its goal? Richard Hansen, in a recent preaching article, writes, "As a young preacher, I was certain that if I marshaled enough exegetical evidence (from the original languages, of course), I could bludgeon my listeners into belief. My sermons were like boxing matches; I didn't always score a knockout, but I expected to win on points."[7] The preacher who does not take into account these realities will find that his approach is much like talking to a wall or punching an immovable object.[8]

Postmodern Suspicion

A second obstacle the preacher faces is a general sense of suspicion that pervades contemporary western culture. This is not a failure to trust in God *per se*, but a posture of suspicion indicative of Western culture, now critical of grand truth claims. Middleton and Walsh write that many "have come to the bewildering conclusion or at least the troubling suspicion, that the sure, absolutist claims of modernity are nothing more than historically conditioned conventions, of no more intrinsic worth than the conventions of non-Western or pre-modern cultures."[9] The challenge for the preacher is to commend the gospel to a listener that is influenced by this posture of suspicion. How does the preacher preach the grand truth claim of the

---

6. Lakoff, *Don't Think of an Elephant*, 17

7. Hansen, "Playful Preacher," 211.

8. For more information on the intersection of preaching and modern neuroscience see Cox, *Rewiring Your Preaching*.

9. Middleton and Walsh, *Truth*, 29.

lordship of Jesus Christ to those that believe the Christian metanarrative is really just a cleverly disguised power play?

The preacher who is not cognizant of these obstacles but continually comes armed with proof texts and foolproof arguments Sunday after Sunday will soon find his voice echoing only in the minds of the faithful, while those most in need of the gospel will have had their suspicions confirmed and their cognitive frames reinforced. If the preacher is to make an impact on the congregation, he will have to disarm suspicion and engage the neurological frames of the congregation, tapping into their psychological, spiritual, and emotional dimensions through playfulness, humor, and irony, which is grounded in a comic vision of the Bible.

The Playful Preacher

If we are to be heard in our postmodern context, the preacher must learn to box like Mohammed Ali—floating like a butterfly and stinging like a bee. For the congregation to be challenged, the preacher cannot come banging on the front door of the hearer's home, but instead, like a perpetrator, must cleverly sneak around the side of the house and climb in the back window. The hearer's defenses must be circumvented in order to gain a hearing for the gospel, and this happens through humor and playfulness. Chuck Sackett said it well—that a "good preacher gets the congregation laughing and then slits their throats."

Playfulness disarms the hearer and builds an emotional connection between the preacher and the congregation, which creates openness to the subject. George Bernard Shaw who understood this when he said, "If you are going to tell people the truth, you'd better make them laugh; otherwise they'll kill you."[10] This is the reality every communicator of the gospel faces each Sunday. It is dangerous and politically incorrect to tell every person in the room that he or she is a sinner in need of God's grace and that Jesus Christ is the Lord of the Universe, and so playfulness needs to be employed. Not only does playfulness disarm the hearer, it creates a new dynamic in the preacher. Following Friedman,[11] Hansen argues that when the preacher is playful and lighthearted it frees him up from trying so hard to make an impact, and the emotional triangle between the preacher, message, and congregation changes; people are free to hear what is being said without

10. The quote is disputed as it does not come from any of Shaw's works.

11. Friedman, *Generation to Generation*, 51–52

engaging their defenses.[12] By being playful, the preacher becomes the perpetrator, sneaking around the side of the house and comes in the back door with the challenging message of the Gospel.

The Bible's Comic Vision

Playfulness, however, is not just a clever strategy of preaching, as if preaching was nine-tenths delivery with the Holy Spirit playing a small role, and it is not just telling jokes or being quick-witted. The playfulness of the preacher is grounded in the larger comic vision of the Bible, and by paying attention to the comic elements the preacher can gain the attention of his audience and offer correction and hope. When we understand Scripture as comedy we realize the Bible is also the perpetrator sneaking in the back window and catching us unaware. The kind of playfulness I mean is one that requires deep study of the Scripture in order to help the congregation see how their life fits into its comedy.

Biblical studies professor J. William Whedbee suggests four characteristics of comedy. First, comedies contain U-shaped plotlines, which generally feature a harmonious setting, which is put at risk, but an upswing in fortune is realized in the end. Second, we find a rash of character types: buffoons, rogues, fools, simpletons, and clowns. Third, we see linguistic and stylistic habits and strategies such as punning, irony, wordplay, parody, hyperbole, reversal, and surprise.[13] Whedbee writes, "comedy celebrates the rhythm of life with its times of festivities and joyous renewal, but it must frequently resort to ridicule in order to bring down the arrogant and the boastful who block or threaten the free movement of life."[14] Fourth, comedy functions to conserve social norms and paradoxically to subvert them. When comedy preserves social norms, it uses satire to unmask the forces threatening to undermine those norms. When comedy is subverting the norm or status quo it takes a shot at oppressive and tyrannical realities in society so new social norms can bring freedom and life. In this respect it is revolutionary.[15]

---

12. Hansen, "Playful Preacher," 211.

13. Whedbee, *Bible and the Comic Vision*, 7–10.

14. Ibid., 9

15. For additional resources see Lowery, *Homiletical Plot*; Edwards, *Effective First-Person Biblical Preaching*; Mathewson, *Art of Preaching*.

With this understanding of comedy in hand we see how the Scripture can be described as comedy, not just in a few constituent parts, but as a whole, possessing a grand comic vision. The broad story of redemption featuring a good creation threatened by sin, but redeemed by God's suffering, dying, and rising Messiah is the grandest U-shaped plot we know. In the various stories that comprise the larger narrative we find rogues, buffoons, clowns, simpletons, and tricksters that get it wrong, but are redeemed by God through his grace and mercy. We see irony, as God becomes man—the king taking off his royal robes and taking on the nature of a slave and triumphing through the cross, not the sword. In this story the first will be last and the last will be first. The most stunning display of power is not the coercive action of God in the world, but the surrender of power, God in the flesh, crucified and vindicated in resurrection. These are the great reversals of the Bible and they cut across our human intuitions and ideas about power, empire, and status.

Indeed the Apostle Paul writes: "For the message of the cross is foolishness to those who are perishing, but to us who are being saved it is the power of God. . . . God was pleased through the foolishness of what was preached to save those who believe. . . . For the foolishness of God is wiser than man's wisdom" (1 Cor 1:18, 21, 25, NIV). The humble have been exalted and the exalted humbled; what is foolish in the eyes of the world is wise in the eyes of God. The Bible's comic vision conserves the believing community; it shapes the community and provides identity, but at the same time it subverts the powerful and puts the proud in the shade. This is good news, and wherever the gospel of Jesus is preached it elicits in those who are being saved laughter, wry smiles, and a knowing wink. It is a divine comedy and we've lived it as one of the bumbling characters, but paradoxically have also experienced the hope and joy of the risen Christ as we participate in God's grand reversal.

The preacher in tune with the comic vision of the Bible will humorously connect the buffoonery, deceptiveness, and rebelliousness of the characters with the hope, love, and joy that is found in God's kingdom. As we laugh at the flaws in the characters we see how we have played those same roles in our circles and relationship. We have played the buffoon, we have been threatened, we have experienced great loss, but the story doesn't end as a tragedy, because comedy keeps the believing community hoping. It reminds us that life, though it feels out of control, is U-shaped and the faithful community laughs because they are in on the joke. Comedy says,

"Love wins! Hope wins! God wins!" As Conrad Hyers quips in his book on divine comedy, "where there is humor there is hope, and where there is hope there is humor!"[16]

With this larger comic vision in mind, I want to briefly explore two familiar Biblical texts and the comic elements they contain. Once we have seen how these texts employ these devices I will give some examples of how I've tried to play along with the text in my own preaching. The first example is the abrupt ending of the gospel of Mark and the second is the story of Jonah.

The Ending of Mark

We like the end of a story to resolve conflict, which our contemporary culture reveals in the typical movie ending. Who didn't shed a tear at the end of *Toy Story 3* when everything wraps up nicely and everyone lives happily ever after? Who can resist the temptation to sing along at the end of *The Lego Movie*, "Everything Is Awesome?" Sometimes, however, there are movies that end with cliffhangers like the *Italian Job* or *Inception*. These movies do not bring a final resolution to the characters, though they strive to give enough information for the audience to be confident that the characters will be okay and will get out of the situation that has them presently puzzled. Every once in a while a movie will come along and if the people don't like the ending it's changed.

The movie *Fatal Attraction* had an ending that did not impress test audiences and was later changed. *Fatal Attraction* was a popular movie in 1987 about Dan, his wife Beth, and a woman named Alex. Dan and Alex have a weekend fling, leaving Alex thinking their relationship would progress, but when Dan blows it off, Alex tries to kill his family and is consequently shot to death. Everyone remembers that ending, but the original ending saw Alex commit suicide and frame Dan for murder, but Beth had the evidence to save her husband. Select audiences did not like the ending, so they brought everyone back for filming and gave us the famous bathroom scene.

This brings us to the end of Mark's gospel, which has two alternate endings. It ends on Easter morning with the women arriving at the tomb finding it empty, meeting a young man who tells them to inform the disciples that Jesus has gone ahead of them to Galilee. The last line reads, "Trembling and bewildered, the women went out and fled from the tomb. They said nothing to anyone, because they were afraid" (Mark 16:8). Now,

---

16. Hyers, *And God Created Laughter*, 5.

depending on your translation, there are two different endings, one long and one short, but neither original to the Gospel. They were added later, because the early church was uncomfortable with the way Mark ended. They wanted an ending that wrapped everything up nicely, so they changed it.[17]

It is possible and desirable to see verse 8 as the intentional, ironic, and challenging ending of the Gospel, consistent with the rest of the book of Mark. Irony is regularly employed in the Gospel as a way of drawing the hearer onto the side of the narrator, so he can catch them unaware at the very end. For instance, Mark tells us about Jesus being mocked as the "King of the Jews." His enemies mean it as an insult, but the hearers know that ironically Jesus' enemies are speaking the truth about him. The narrator has let the hearer "in on the full story" so that now the narrator and the audience understand what the mocking characters do not. Rhoads, Dewey, and Michie, in their important work on Mark, write, "and because the audience understands what the characters do not, the audience is led to be on the inside, perhaps even to feel superior to the characters."[18] Once the audience feels superior to the characters the trap has been set for the end of the Gospel, where Mark ironically plays off previous episodes to pose a challenging question to his audience. Two stories help Mark set his trap.

In Mark 5:21–43 a leader of the local synagogue named Jairus comes to Jesus requesting his help in healing his daughter, but as Jesus is on the way to see her they are interrupted and the little girl dies during the delay. Jesus continues on his way to the home of Jairus despite the news of her death, and upon arrival sends everyone out of the room. He speaks to the little girl and she gets up and starts walking around. Jesus instructs those there to get her something to eat (because apparently being resurrected works up an appetite) and gives everyone strict orders not to tell anyone about the miracle.

Similarly, in 7:31–37, when Jesus is traveling through the Decapolis, the people bring him a blind and mute man. They beg Jesus to lay his hand on him. Jesus takes him away from the crowd, puts his fingers in the man's ears, spits, and touches the man's tongue. He looks towards the heavens and then with a groan, says, "Be opened." Immediately the man can hear and speak plainly. After the healing has occurred, "Jesus commanded them not to tell anyone. But the more he did so, the more they kept talking about

17. For more information on the ending of Mark see Evans, *Mark 8:27–16:20*, 540–551.

18. Rhoads, Dewey, and Michie, *Mark As Story*, 60.

it."[19] The people are amazed at what Jesus has done, and the more Jesus instructs them to keep quiet the more zealous they are in proclaiming it to their friends.

Six times Jesus tells people not to say anything about his miracles, and the people never listen. Mark goes out of his way to point out that the more Jesus told people to be quiet the more the people continued to announce his deeds from the rooftops. The only characters in the gospel that are obedient to this command are the demons. Finally, at the end, Jesus has performed the most amazing miracle of all—he has been raised from the dead. The climactic moment has finally arrived that Jesus had told his disciples about multiple times, and now that the time has arrived, what do they do? They don't tell anyone! They run away scared!

Mark, who has set the trap for the hearers, making them feel superior to the characters, now challenges the unsuspecting audience to preach the gospel and not to run away scared. Rhoads, Dewey, and Michie write, "the ironic ending of Mark . . . punctures any self-confident superiority the audience might have, for the ending turns irony back upon the audience. . . . The irony perpetrated on the audience becomes a challenge to proclaim the good news courageously in the face of persecution rather than be silent."[20] Mark doesn't resolve the story, because the story isn't resolved until the hearer decides for himself if they will meet up with Jesus in Galilee and tell the story of his resurrection. The original audience hearing Mark as an oral performance, of course, knew that the women did tell. How else would they be in a position to experience it? But the hearer nods and says, "I see what you did there," and now must decide what they will do in light of the resurrected Lord Jesus.

The Comedy of Jonah

The book of Jonah is another good example of biblical comedy that draws the hearer into the story and then surprisingly challenges strict Israelite nationalism. The hearer is meant to identify with Jonah and to see his or her own flaws reflected in Jonah's. Conrad Hyers writes, "When we look at the figure of Jonah, his self-centeredness and narrow-mindedness, his extreme behavior, his self-contradictions, we laugh at him and, as we laugh,

19. Mark 7:36, NIV.
20. Rhoads, Dewey, and Michie, *Mark As Story*, 60.

realize that we are laughing at ourselves."[21] The story of Jonah contains many points of irony, humor, surprise, and reversal. We begin with Jonah's name. He is Jonah, son of Amittai, which means son of faithfulness. We know from 2 Kings 14:25 that Jonah was a hero of his time. The texts tells us that Jeroboam II "was the one who restored the boundaries of Israel from Lebo Amath to the Sea of the Arabah, in accordance with the word of the LORD, the God of Israel spoken through his servant Jonah son of Amittai, the prophet from Gath Hepher."[22] Jereboam II, who was not a faithful king, listens to Jonah and together they usher in the longest and final period of peace in the Northern Kingdom of Israel. Jonah was the kind of prophet that could keep his head down and be faithful in spite of a king who has generally been unfaithful to the Lord. He is the perfect prophet to send to Assyria, the son of faithfulness.

However, Jonah does not want to go to Nineveh, because he knows that Yahweh is compassionate and slow to anger and might extend sympathy to the Ninevites. So he runs in the opposite direction and hops on board a boat going in the opposite direction of Nineveh. While he is at sea a great storm comes up, and as the sailors are crying out to their gods, Jonah is asleep below the deck. The captain comes in and asks Jonah to call out to his God, but instead Jonah convinces the sailors to throw him overboard, for he is at fault for the storm. The sailors throw him overboard, which calms the storm, and the sailors sacrifice and make vows to Jonah's God. Jonah is swallowed by a fish, prays to God, and is vomited up on land. Once he towels off, he goes to Nineveh, preaches the message, and all the peoples and their beasts put on sackcloth. This makes Jonah angry, so he storms out of town, picks a spot where he can watch their destruction, and throws a temper tantrum over a dead gourd.

Jonah the son of faithfulness gets shown up by the faithless, he tries to run away from his God who can't be escaped, he is oblivious to the concerns of Yahweh, and would rather die than witness God's mercy revealed to those he deems unworthy. He preaches the shortest and lamest sermon in the Bible. "Forty more days and Nineveh will be overturned," which is actually vague, since the word overturned can mean "destruction," or "changed," or "transformed."[23] So Jonah preaches a lame, short, vague

21. Hyers, God Created Laughter, 96.

22. 2 Kings 14:25, NIV.

23. No doubt Jonah had destruction on his mind, while Yahweh had transformation on his. For more information on "overturned" see NIDOTTE, s.v. "הפך" 1048.

sermon and 120,000 people respond with repentance, the best response to a sermon in the whole Bible.

At the center of the story we find Jonah in the belly of the fish. He has "gone down" to Joppa, down below deck, down into the sea, and down into the belly of the fish, and Jonah prays. He does not repent or acknowledge his disobedience. He prays the classical, "Lord, if you get me out of this mess I promise I'll . . ." kind of prayer.[24] The Lord hears his cry and the last line of the prayer is the theological center of the book: deliverance belongs to the Lord. Indeed, deliverance belongs to God, and he saves Jonah and, he saves Nineveh, because deliverance belongs to God, even if Jonah's actions contradict the theological center of the book and even if Jonah is in the innermost place of *Sheol*.

And just like that God commands the fish and Jonah is vomited out onto dry land. The Hebrew word for vomit is like someone who has gorged himself and relieves himself by vomiting. Jonah is covered in fish guts, slime, seaweed, and whatever else that fish had managed to swallow. It's a hilarious moment. Phillip Carey writes in his commentary on Jonah:

> Jonah's actual escape from the depths is a ridiculous anticlimax, not a dramatic rescue, but a bit of indigestion. It is as if Jonah made the monster sick to its stomach. It would be nice if the belly of *Sheol* worked like that. And perhaps it does, thanks to the word of the Lord. Will we all laugh as we emerge from our graves on the last day? Will we be astounded as we blink and look around at ourselves? We thought death was so serious, but look at this silly mess! Time to clean up all the dirt and fish guts—yes, and let's get those grave clothes off Lazarus—it's all too funny looking for words![25]

The regurgitation scene is a hilarious moment in the story because it reminds us that joy is just around the corner; when you are going down into the pit, into the heart of *Sheol*, God finds us there and delivers us. Joy wins! Hope wins! God wins! These problems, like Nineveh and fish, cancer, or divorce, seem like huge, insurmountable problems, but are not really problems for God, and ultimately are not problems for those who know his deliverance. For one greater than Jonah has come and he "descends [into *Sheol*] not as a rebel fleeing from God but as the word of God in the flesh, as hell's conqueror not its victim."[26] Death could not contain him and it has

---

24. See Brueggemann, *Great Prayers*, 58–67.

25. Cary, *Jonah*, 104.

26. Ibid.

no power over anyone who has life in his name. The faithful community can laugh and find strength in the Lord's joy, because we are in on the joke; we know death doesn't have the last word—deliverance belongs to the Lord, and he rescues those who call out to him.

Comedy & Preaching

So how does a preacher grounded in the comic vision of the Bible playfully engage the congregation with the texts discussed above? Here are a few examples of how I have tried to accomplish this in my own preaching. At the start of 2014 I wanted to challenge the congregation to live "On Mission," so I decided to preach the ending of Mark. I started the sermon by mentioning several movie endings that have a happy ending and resolve the conflict by the end of the film, like *Toy Story 3*. Then I showed a clip of the 1969 *Italian Job* ending that is literally a cliffhanger. From there we read the end of Mark and stopped at verse 8. I spent a few minutes explaining the manuscript issues and went on to suggest that if verse 8 was the original ending, it is brilliantly done.

I then told the two miracle stories discussed earlier in this essay, which include Jesus performing a miracle, the people being told to keep quiet about it, and everyone telling the story anyway. I played on those stories for a while, telling contemporary stories about how people can't keep their mouths shut, even when they are sworn to secrecy. Not only is this true of secrets, but it is often the way people respond to a rule; we want to contradict what we've been told. A former office manager at our church put a label on our stapler that said, "Do not remove stapler from office." The label took up the entire length of the stapler. Every time I saw that stapler I just wanted to pick it up and walk around the building with it. This is just the way it is with people, as soon as we are told a thing is forbidden, we cannot be happy unless we can carry on with what is not allowed. I wanted the congregation to laugh at the characters, maybe feel a little superior to them, but to see how those same tendencies play out in our own lives.

From there, I went back to the ending of Mark and pointed out that no one can keep their mouth shut about the miracles of Jesus when he asked them to keep it a secret, but when the climax of the Christ event was upon them and they are supposed to go and tell, they run away frightened, not saying a word to anyone. The ending is a cliffhanger because it wants you and me to see that "we have told" when we were supposed to be quiet and "ran away scared" when we've been commanded to "go and tell." Mark ends abruptly because the Gospel isn't finished until you and I decide to meet Jesus in Galilee; it doesn't resolve until we announce it to all nations. From there I went on to challenge the congregation to live "On Mission" this year and to fill in the blank Mark has left for us. I have preached sermons and entire series on "sharing your faith" and many of them have been practical and helpful to members of our congregation, but sometimes the message to "preach the gospel" can become so common that people tune it out. The ironic ending of Mark allowed me to preach a familiar topic, but sneak in through the back window at the end with the challenging punch line.[27]

I recently completed a four-part series on the book of Jonah, one week for each chapter. Since the book of Jonah is so short it's easier to see all the points of irony and then playfully point them out over a period of four weeks. The first week I titled my sermon "Son of Faithfulness" and played up the heroism of Jonah during Jereboam's reign. Then I went into a summary of the story and played on the irony of the son of faithfulness getting shown up by all the faithless pagans in the story. The second week, I played on the theme of Jonah going down, but when he has hit rock bottom he finds the deliverance of God. At the center of the sermon I highlighted the regurgitation scene. I pointed out the Hebrew word was not spit, but vomit. This is not a fish just spitting Jonah onto land; this fish has just been to a Chinese buffet. I have never walked out of a Chinese buffet and said, "I'm a genius!" This fish disgorges itself and Jonah comes out covered in seaweed, fish guts, and half-chewed fish food smeared all over his face. We laughed about anyone on the shore that day that might have witnessed the event and what Jonah must have looked like. I went on to play up all the other funny moments in the whole book, and made the point that the funny moments at the end of Jonah's distress remind us that when we are going down, when we have hit rock bottom, God is there doing something great. The vomit scene reminds us that joy and laughter are just around the corner.

The final sermon I did was the most playful of them all. Each week I had covered significant exegetical details in each chapter, summarized the whole story when relevant, and connected the story to the sign of Jonah in the New Testament. So the last week I wanted to finish it off with a humorous and creative telling of the whole story. I decided a first person narrative would be the best choice, so I was the worm in the story, who had been

27. For an additional resource on preaching and the Gospel of Mark see Blount and Charles, *Preaching Mark.*

living in Joppa, but hitched a ride in Jonah's bag. When we got to Nineveh I didn't know much about Jonah's God so when all the other animals put on sackcloth and fasted, so did I. Well, by the middle of the night I got so hungry that I couldn't stand it any longer, I crawled out of Jonah's bag, inched down to the vine that had provided shade for Jonah's head and smote it with my mighty jaws, gorging myself on it until I lay there on the ground like a python who had just swallowed a pig. I kept my identity a secret through most of the sermon, dropping hints along the way, until I broke my fast with the divine vine. I crafted the worm character to care mostly about himself, mirroring Jonah's concerns, which stood out in stark contrast to the concerns of God throughout the book. This was a creative way for me to tell the story I had been telling the last three weeks and pose the final question at the end of the Jonah to the congregation.

Conclusion

The Bible is a divine comedy and it draws us into its comic vision on every page. The characters make us laugh at ourselves, its revolutionary message cuts us to the heart, and its joy forms, shapes, and gives identity to our communal life through its hope-filled message of the resurrected Jesus. The wise, playful preacher will follow the Bible's lead, letting the text win by drawing the listener into the Bible's comic vision, bypassing the hearer's defenses so the message of the gospel can sneak in the back window and transform them. The Bible calls us into the story. It challenges us to write our own verse and to participate in the grand reversal of God. Good preaching will model the reality of the Bible and call the hearer out of the crowd and onto the stage, not as a spectator but as an actor caught up in the grand drama of God.

7

Microscope and Telescope
How Expositional Preaching
Grows into Theological Arc

MARK SCOTT

Introduction

SOME PREACHERS HAVE STRONGER handshakes than others.[1] Their grips are capable of squeezing a text and getting more out of it than others. These preachers can leverage more out of a text than others. They ask better questions of the text and see more in a text than others. Preachers with these strong grips go further than others, and the text sings and dances powerfully.[2]

Why? It could be that some are gifted by God. After all, teaching is a spiritual gift (Rom 12:7b; 1 Cor 12:28; Eph 4:11; 1 Pet 4:11). It could be that some have a stronger sense of calling (Isa 6:8; Jer 1:4–5; Acts 26:16–18). It could be that some are just brighter. Let's face it: mental acumen is not

---

1. Of course I am speaking metaphorically. A firm or soft handshake might tell psychologists volumes about a preacher's personality. But I am speaking about a preacher's grip on the text to be preached.

2. My dear friend and classmate, Chuck Sackett, does all of this. He can find the text's full significance, and the listener says, "That was rich." They feel informed, blessed, and convicted. And this is true down to his illustrations. When you hear Chuck preach, you know the message will be very well prepared and you will discern that everything possible came from that text. The text won.

distributed equally. Some preachers have ACT scores that are off the charts. Other preachers are not the brightest crayons in the box.[3] Other preachers might be more yielding to the Holy Spirit. One preacher said, "The Holy Spirit won't manifest himself until we deny ourselves." Some preachers might be given different opportunities, and those opportunities will stretch them farther. Finally, some preachers have been, in the providence of God, given a chance for more thorough preparation.

A gifted expositor, like Chuck Sackett, will always ask each text, "What do you have to say about Jesus?" God's big story (metanarrative) should never be neglected while preaching the little stories (petite narratives) from this huge canon. The canon is fixed, but the document is living. And the best way the preacher can make it live week in and week out is to ensure that Jesus is not marginalized and that the plan of God to save the world and move creation to new creation is not compromised. Chuck balances the microscope and telescope, exemplifying the theological arc described in this chapter.

Lots of Good Things to Preach from the Bible

The Bible offers much in terms of preaching.[4] The edifying things that could be shared from Scripture are truly ginormous. For instance, who doesn't enjoy preaching about *family life* from Genesis (although John Ortberg says that those people clearly need a therapist) and the Epistles? Who doesn't thrill with *liberation themes* from Exodus or personal *piety* from Leviticus? *Biblical justice* themes seem to exude from Exodus and Deuteronomy. Joshua and Acts are full of *missions*. Where can you find a better

---

3. I hope this doesn't sound overly harsh. The fact of the matter is that the God of the Bible is attracted to weakness. One of the great subthemes of the Bible is *power through seeming weakness*. Preachers who feel that they were overlooked when the Creator passed out brains should take heart that God is able to bring down the mighty and the intelligent through seeming weakness (Isa 57:15; 1 Cor 1:18–21).

4. There is no space here to insert a theology of preaching. But, in my opinion, the Bible was intended from the very beginning to be a preaching/speaking book. The events of the Bible happened first (except for predictive prophecy). Then inspired writers wrote down what happened. But, those writers wrote down what happened in such a way that the events, in a sense, happened again. In other words, what was written down was written down in such a way as to be spoken again. Old Testament preaching consisted of *explaining* the law in terms of redemption from exile in the context of covenant community. New Testament preaching consisted of the good news *announcement* that God had come in Christ and was reestablishing his reign.

love story than Ruth and Song of Songs? Preachers have extrapolated *financial principles* from Proverbs. *Leadership themes* pour out over Nehemiah and the Pastoral Epistles. The Gospels are full of teaching on *discipleship,* while Psalms and Revelation can take our *worship* to another level.

Preachers want to help their people, and themes such as financial principles and piety *do* help. There is nothing sinful about a preacher helping angry people get a grip on their tempers. Many a Christian parent would be blessed to learn what the Bible says about proper parenting. Some of the "Eeyores" in the church could use a biblical prescription for having a more positive outlook, and some Christians would profit by learning how to handle their finances better. However, Jesus was not some kind of itinerant therapist who went around helping people feel better.[5] In fact, he often made them feel worse (Mark 10:22). Many people who invited Jesus home for dinner were made to feel more than a little uncomfortable (Luke 7:36–50; 14:7–11).

But Something is Missing . . . The Big Story

I wonder if deep down preachers know when they preach sermons like those mentioned above that they have cheated their congregations. While it feels ministerially satisfying to meet people at the point of their need, preachers are not totally satisfied with that kind of preaching. Something is missing, and preachers owe the church more. Remaining at the point of their need doesn't meet the larger needs of the people. Worse yet, many allegorize the text and make the Bible say something that it does not say.[6]

The thesis and conviction of this chapter is that expositional/textual preaching loses the proverbial forest for the trees. How can preachers do the wonderful analytical work on the text and not lose Scripture's metanarrative? Even more, how can preachers allow their microscopic work on individual texts to grow into the telescopic big lens of God's plan to save the world through Jesus and move creation to new creation? That takes additional effort and reflection.

---

5. He did go about doing good (Acts 10:38), but that is different than helping people be happy, happy, happy.

6. It may be true that some preachers are oblivious to this. They don't even seem to be conscious about such mishandling of the Word of God. By "allegorizing" I mean assigning meaning to the text that was not intended.

The complete expository preacher will want exposition to grow into theological arc.[7] Expositors never want to lose the big story of God's plan to unite all things in Christ (Eph 1:9–10), regardless of what their text is. The effects are serious when preachers don't pay attention to Scripture's metanarrative, the theological arc. Jesus gets marginalized, the kingdom gets avoided, and viewing salvation as the healing of all creation gets only a passing glance.[8] Dr. Wayne Shaw reminds us, "If Christ isn't in it, then it isn't a Christian sermon." Albert Mohler reminds us, "All Christian preaching is unabashedly Christological."[9] Robert Smith reminds us that the Bible is "Himbook."[10] Smith develops the idea that the expositor is an exegetical escort ushering the hearers into the presence of God for the purpose of transformation.[11] Finally, H. H. Farmer said, "The preacher may present a charming and literate discourse, but . . . because it does not offer the life of God in Christ, it suffers the same fate as the seed sown on rocky soil."[12]

In the earliest days of the New Testament this big story emphasis was firmly in place. The Synoptics, John, the Epistles, and Revelation all bear witness to this. When Jesus exposed Isa 61 in the Nazareth synagogue (Luke 4:16–30) he used two Old Testament narratives to illustrate his point, but he also claimed messianic fulfillment. That is, the Christ factor and the Jesus connection were there. When Jesus walked on the Road to Emmaus with the two disciples, he "interpreted" and "opened" the Scriptures concerning himself (Luke 24:27, 35, 44).[13] In his famous sermon on his deity and credentials, Jesus said that the Scriptures, rightly understood, spoke of him (John 5:39).

---

7. An arc is anything shaped like a bow, curve, or arch. It is a segment of a curve, used primarily in geometry or electricity. An equally good term would be "arch." An arch is a structural device forming the curved, pointed, or flat upper edge of an opening or support as on a bridge or doorway. Either way, preachers should want their expositions to grow into something bigger than just their text itself.

8. To ensure that these important things don't get lost we are using the imagery of microscope and telescope in this chapter. Exposition demands one (microscope), and theology demands the other (telescope).

9. Mohler, "Theology of Preaching," 16.

10. Smith, *Doctrine That Dances*, 100.

11. Ibid, 25.

12. Lischer, *Theology of Preaching*, 14.

13. Both the words for hermeneutics and exegesis are used in Luke 24, but they end up being in service to the *person* of Christ.

Paul is likewise constrained. While marking out the blessings that believers have in Christ, Paul says that God's eternal plan was to sum up all things under the headship of Christ (Eph 1:9–10). Is preaching included in the "all things" of that passage? Then, previous to his second prayer in the book of Ephesians he states that God's wisdom (plan?) is made known through the church (Eph 3:10). How else would this be known without proclamation? In the twin Epistles to the Ephesians, Paul states that the ultimate goal of his teaching and admonishing is to present every person mature in Christ (Col 1:28).

Even in John's Revelation, the end of time is announced this way: "the kingdom of the world will become the kingdom of our God and his Christ, and he shall reign forever and forever" (Rev 11:15, ESV). It would seem then that the major sweeps of genre in the New Testament underscore the significance of telling the big story while doing exposition on the little stories of the Bible.

Examples That Ignore the Theological Arc

A very fine sermon was preached by Erwin McManus in *Preaching Today*.[14] It concerned Jonathan and his armor bearer climbing up a hill and attacking the Philistines. From that Old Testament text McManus extrapolated several principles about church leadership: trusting God against incredible odds and walking by faith. It is a very fine sermon. But a weakness is that it bore very little witness to God's plan to save the world through Christ.[15] It missed the theological arc.

Another good message was preached by Louie Giglio at the North American Christian Convention in Phoenix.[16] The title of the message was, "Moses, the Little Leader." The text was Exod 3–4. He stressed that Moses, instead of being a gargantuan leader, was actually quite a little leader

14. McManus, "Seizing Your Divine Moment."

15. Preaching Christ from the Old Testament can be challenging indeed. Preaching Christ from Old Testament narratives can be even more challenging. Many of us have been blessed by Fee and Stuart, *How to Read the Bible for All Its Worth*. In the chapter on Hebrew narrative (78–93) they stress the three levels of those narratives. The bottom level concerns the basic moral meaning of the story—which, in this case, McManus did a wonderful job of illuminating. The next level concerns what the story meant to Israel. How would it have advanced the chosen people? The final (top) level concerned how the story fits into God's plan to save the world.

16. Giglio, "Moses."

compared to Yahweh. So powerful was this message that people went out and put a line from his message—I am not, but I know I AM—on T-shirts that week. But a weakness was that it failed to show how Moses was a type of Christ, how he would lead the people out of the bondage and exile, and that the remnant would be saved so Christ could come and save the world.

I once preached a sermon from Jer 35 about the Rechabites. God told Jeremiah a very strange thing. He urged the weeping prophet to bring the Rechabite family into one of the side rooms of the temple and set wine before them. God knew that the Rechabite family wouldn't drink wine because they followed in the ways of their father Jonadab, who taught his family, among other things, not to drink. God uses this as an illustration of how a covenant family listened to their father, whereas the children of Israel wouldn't listen to their heavenly Father. I was able to preach about the leaving of a family legacy and the importance of God's Word in our families. But at the end of the day, I knew I neglected something. Indeed, God was giving his people an object lesson, but he also wanted them to be faithful to God by listening to his word as they headed off to captivity so that the remnant could be preserved and Christ could come through the seed of Abraham.

Hitting the Bull's-Eye of the Theological Arc

So what are preachers to do? How can preachers ensure that their expositions are Christ-centered and hit the bull's-eye of the big story of Scripture? Here are some approaches to consider. First, let *words* help. Sometimes the words of the texts themselves will offer direct statements that take the exposition to theology. Think of Paul saying, "This is a faithful saying deserving full acceptance, that Christ Jesus came into the world to save sinners, of whom I am foremost of all" (1 Tim 1:15). That's hard to miss. The direct word is always best. But even an Old Testament word can do this. The book of Ruth is a prime example. One could suggest that Boaz is a type of Christ, but a more direct *word* link would be the word "kinsman-redeemer" (*gō'ēl*). The narrative rises to a climax with this word. Once it appears in Ruth 2:20, it occurs many times by the end of the book. Words take the preacher to theological arc.

Second, let *layers of literary context* help. The Bible is much like the city of Jerusalem. It has layers and layers of foundations. Rachel, Jacob's favorite wife, died near Bethlehem. Centuries later when the Israelites were being carried off into Babylonian captivity, it was as if Rachel came forth from her grave and wept as the children of Israel headed to Babylon. Matthew makes a typological connection of Rachel coming forth from her grave again as Herod, the Butcher of Bethlehem, kills the innocent children of the area in Ramah. The story is intended to do more than make us weep (though that is no small thing). It is intended to remind us that as terrible as the children dying was, a certain child was rescued and fled to Egypt, and he will usher in a new way to be right with God. Sometimes layers of context (and maybe typology) take us to theological arc.

Third, let *parallel stories* help. This is especially true when dealing with Hebrew narratives. These could be viewed as redemptive analogies. Judah's touching speech to Joseph about substituting his life for that of Benjamin might qualify (Gen 44:32).[17] Think about Nehemiah "going up" to Jerusalem to inspect the walls. Does it sound familiar to the travel narrative of Luke? Jesus is always "going up to Jerusalem" (Luke 9:51—19:28). Sometimes parallel stories take us to theological arc.

Fourth, let the *lectionary* or *Christian calendar* help. Matching text and calendar, since God created both,[18] can create a different hearing of a passage. Certain texts will receive a meaningful hearing with certain theological underpinnings when they are heard on certain days. A text that might not seem all that theologically bent may take on theological overtones when heard on Christmas or Easter.[19] The lectionary or Christian calendar takes us to the theological arc.

Fifth, let *historical background* help. Because the Bible did not take place in a vacuum, historical context matters. Even in one of Jesus' most famous parables, the parable of the Prodigal Son, there is some profound theology.[20] Luke 15:20 is one of the finest descriptions of the love of God

---

17. This is the story that sends Joseph over the emotional edge. Joseph has to leave the room to gain his composure. Keep another connection in mind as well. Jesus is from the tribe of Judah. The language of Judah's speech reminds one of the substitutionary nature of Jesus' death on the cross.

18. At least God carved time out of eternity (not necessarily the calendar *per se*).

19. This idea of hearing certain passages on certain days has a rich past that precedes the Christian era. Our Jewish forefathers read certain portions of the Old Testament at certain festivals of their faith. The festival gave theological context to the text.

20. This statement will not resonate with all readers. Some are persuaded that parables are merely illustrations and should not be pressed into "doctrinal" service. But do the parables say nothing to us about the nature of God or the love of Christ? Jesus used many parables in his teaching. Why would it seem odd for him to put his theology into story form? Isn't that what the Bible is—a redemptive story?

in story form: "But while he was still a long way off, his father saw him and felt compassion, and ran and embraced him and kissed him." To know the backdrop of parables and to know certain historical details of that day can be theologically helpful.[21] Historical background can take us to the theological arc.

Sixth, let *antecedent theology* or *eschatology* help. In other words, think forward and think backward in the Bible's progressive revelation. While it might be most respectful to read the Bible forward before we read it backward, both directions help theological understanding. In other words, when exposing one portion of Scripture, think of former events, people, or things that circle back to former theological significance. An example of this might be Luke 9:57–62. Jesus encounters three "would-be" disciples. He mentions the place of saying good-bye to family and putting one's hand to the plow for the sake of the kingdom of God. Might this be an allusion to the Elijah and Elisha narrative of 1 Kgs 19:19–21? When Elijah calls Elisha into prophetic service, Elisha wants to go back and say good-bye to his family, and he happens to be plowing at the time of the call. More than a coincidence? Consider Gen 22:1–19. While preachers should be cautious of borrowing too much freight of later revelation to interpret Abraham's willingness to offer Isaac as a sacrifice, who can deny the parallels of another father with another son on another day? Antecedent theology or eschatology can take us to the theological arc.

Seventh, let *exile and remnant thinking* help. One of the great themes of Scripture is that God is always bringing his people out of exile. It can be Egypt, Babylon, or sin—it matters not. God's people are always pilgrims, aliens, and strangers in this world. God is always bringing them out of captivity to new life and covenant. God is always preserving for himself a remnant through whom he will act to reestablish his reign on the earth. We talk about dying and going to heaven. The Bible has more to say about heaven coming here through Christ and God's reign being realized in a new social reality on earth. Whenever preaching on texts about the "kingdom of God coming near" in the Gospels, this theological nuance could be noted. Exile and remnant thinking will take us to the theological arc.

Eighth, let watching the *promise* or *God-talk* help. When preaching from the Old Testament a good question to ask is, "What is happening to

---

21. For more on how parables can inform us theologically see Blomberg, *Interpreting the Parables*; Bailey, *Poet and Peasant* and *Through Peasant Eyes*; Snodgrass, *Stories with Intent*.

the promise of Gen 12:3?" Is it being advanced? Is it being compromised? Is it being challenged? What is happening to the promise to save the world through Jesus? When preaching from the New Testament a good question to ask is, "Where is the God-talk?"[22] For instance, in the parable (?) of Lazarus and the Rich Man (Luke 16:19–31), where is the God-talk? Is it significant that Lazarus is named in this parable? Is it significant that Lazarus is the New Testament name for Eliezer in the Old Testament? Is it significant that Abraham had a servant named Eliezer? Typical to the rabbinic parables of Jesus' day, fathers, kings, and landowners played a God role in the stories. In this parable so does Abraham. Taking note of the promise or God-talk can take us to the theological arc.

Ninth, let *genre* help. Of course the Bible is a kaleidoscope of genre. Paying attention not only to "what" the text says but also "how" the text says it will pay rich dividends for the preacher and keep the preacher theologically in place. Redemptive analogies have already been mentioned with regard to Hebrew narrative. Also, several New Testament genres have already been mentioned. But the legal genre (constitutional literature), wisdom genre, prophetic genre, and poetic genre also, by their nature, speak of God's plan to save the world.

The legal genre drives us to Christ. Probe the precepts of the legal genre, and Jesus emerges. Behind the *precept* is a *principle*. Behind the *principle* is the *person* of God. God said, "Do not steal" (Exod 20:15). What is behind that precept? Isn't it the principle of generosity? God desires that his people be givers, not takers (2 Cor 9:7). But what lies behind that principle? Isn't it the person (character) of God? God himself is a giver.

The wisdom genre drives us to Jesus. Wisdom literature is the backstage pass to the Bible. It may not speak of Jesus directly in so many places, but it underlines our *need* for Jesus. It doesn't argue—it asserts. It's true in its context. That is why it can sound so upside down in places.[23]

Prophetic genre drives us to Jesus. Of course predictive prophecy comes to mind. When the expositor notices this in the text it is joy unspeakable. Things like the virgin birth (Isa 7:14), the Son of David (2 Sam

22. By "God talk" I mean where the person or work of the Triune God appears in the text.

23. Apparent contradictions abound in wisdom literature. It should be remembered that, hermeneutically speaking, a proverb (for instance) is always true—but only in its context. For instance, Prov 26:4 says that we are not to answer a fool according to his folly. But the very next verse says that we are to answer a fool according to his folly (26:5). Both verses, side by side, while sounding contradictory, are actually true—in their contexts.

7:12), the king riding into Jerusalem on a donkey (Zech 9:9), and God's servant suffering beyond measure (Isa 53:4–5) all point us directly to Jesus.

In addition to predictive prophecy there is the backdrop of *exile* in prophetic literature. This has already been addressed above. But the prophets can clearly be divided as preexilic, exilic, and postexilic. The exile to Babylon was the defining point historically and theologically in the Old Testament.[24]

Finally, the poetic genre drives us to Jesus. Seth Wilson used to say, "As the soul is caught up in the wonder of God, the language always approximates that of poetry." How else can we talk about God? We use words, but they become so inadequate to speak of God. Even words become metaphors when it comes to talking about the Divine. There is probably as much predictive prophecy about Christ in the Psalms as there is in the books labeled "prophetic." Awareness of genre can take us to the theological arc.

So, sometimes an awareness of genre can take us to theology. These nine approaches function like the roads in England. Spurgeon reminded a young man once that every town, village, and hamlet in England had a road that led to London. A preacher likewise finds the way to Jesus even if he has to go over "hedge and ditch."[25]

A Moving Target and A Final Word

What is being called for in this chapter is not easy. To rightly extrapolate the "Christ event" from an individual text takes experience, awareness, and much study.[26] Developing a theological arc takes much effort. Microscope and telescope have been used in this chapter, as metaphors of the kind of work preachers must do on the text. Most preachers are better at analysis than synthesis. Preachers get the microscope. But allowing that work to

---

24. I want to be kindspirited to my Evangelical friends whose millennial position makes them interpret many Old Testament prophetic passages to refer to the *return* of Christ. They may be correct. But in their original context, those passages are overwhelmingly about the *return* of Israel from captivity.

25. Chapell, *Christ-Centered Preaching*, 280.

26. Smith says, "In an attempt to define doctrinal preaching, the mystery cannot be demystified, and the inscrutable cannot be scrutinized" (*Doctrine*, 30).

grow into a telescopic lens is much more difficult.[27] Biblical scholarship is not static. It keeps moving.[28]

I will side with the Reformers. While being upset with the careless allegorizing done in the medieval church, they chose to allegorize the text only as a last resort. That seems like good advice to me. Sometimes I don't know how to find my way to Jesus in some texts. But since the New Testament seems to operate with a Christ-centered hermeneutic I am committed to doing the same as the Reformers. When all else fails, get to Jesus somehow. Spurgeon said it well: "I take my text and make a beeline to the cross."[29] One day in class Dr. Haddon Robinson said, "Spurgeon preached all the right things from all the wrong texts."[30] The Greeks had it right: "Sir, we would see Jesus" (John 12:21).

27. One thing I know from being an amateur astronomer is that when you fix your telescope to the North Star at night to begin your viewing of the heavens you have to constantly adjust the dials due to the earth's rotation.

28. In church history we have come through the tensions between Antioch and Alexandria on how to interpret the biblical text, generations of allegorical understandings, the historical-grammatical method of interpretation, various criticisms, genre sensitivity, insights from antiquities and archaeology, and all the hermeneutical lenses of the postmodern world as to what texts mean and how they are read.

29. Instead of giving the original quotation from the primary source, I chose to quote it from Proctor, "Beeline to the Cross," 103–121. Matt traces six strategies, which ensure that Jesus makes the sermon 1) watch for the predictions of Christ, 2) the pictures of Christ, 3) the preparation for Christ, 4) the prerequisite for Christ, 5) the presence of Christ, and 6) the provision of Christ.

30. Scott, Class Notes, "Biblical Preaching I."

8

Staying in the Text—Preaching to the Heart
Theological Reflection in Preaching

MARK A. SEARBY

In July 2013, a group of Doctor of Ministry students participated in a seminar which Beeson Divinity School hosted in London, England. One of the highlights of the seminar was the opportunity to spend a morning with Dr. Richard Bewes, former rector of All Souls Church in London. During the session with Dr. Bewes, one of the students asked about his approach to preaching. After a brief pause, Dr. Bewes responded, "It is important to stay with Scripture and to target the heart."[1] A slight paraphrase of his response is the title for this chapter in this book in honor of Chuck Sackett: "Staying in the Text—Preaching to the Heart."

Chuck is a former colleague at Lincoln Christian University and currently teaches regularly in the Doctor of Ministry program at Beeson Divinity School. Our professional and personal friendship extends back to the early 1990s when I served as a trustee at LCU prior to joining the faculty in 1995.

Chuck's preaching is a beautiful model of "staying in the text and preaching to the heart." Through the years I have listened to his preaching many times and have heard him teach about preaching. He is a thoroughly

1. Personal interview with Dr. Richard Bewes, former Rector of All Souls Church in London, England (1983-2004). Conducted at All Souls Church on August 1, 2013.

biblical preacher who captures the meaning of the text and addresses the hearts of his listeners. In the words of David Read, Chuck is "ambidextrous—one arm stretched out in faith grasping the Word of God and the other reaching out in compassion to meet the needs of real people today."

Theological Reflection as Part of the Hermeneutical Work in Preaching

I have listened to many sermons in which it was apparent that the preacher had done much work in the study, exegeting the text and digging for background information. I have heard fewer sermons in which it was obvious that the preacher had reflected upon the text in a way that would allow him to be faithful to the text *and* speak to the congregation in a manner that connected with their hearts. Theological reflection is a much underutilized process in sermon development.

Theological reflection is a Spirit-directed process. It utilizes Scripture as the primary source of authority, recognizes the interpretive value of Christian tradition, and understands that one's life experiences and cultural influences impact one's interpretations of Scripture and tradition. The following diagram illustrates the central work of the Holy Spirit in the process and the ongoing interaction between the other aspects of the reflection process. (This model is shaped by the Wesleyan quadrilateral method.)[2]

2. Cf. Thorsen, *Wesleyan Quadrilateral.*

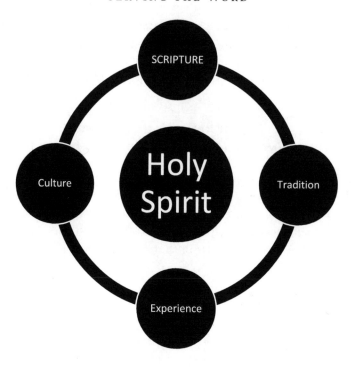

Scripture itself makes it clear that having the Spirit is an essential prerequisite to understanding God's Word (cf. 1 Cor 2:10f). Thus, the Spirit is involved in the preacher's interpretation of Scripture and his reflection upon its truth and application. The student of Scripture must embrace the Spirit's role in inspiration and interpretation—perhaps a more helpful term for the latter is "illumination." Greg Heisler, in his book *Spirit-Led Preaching*, provides a clear distinction between "inspiration" and "illumination":

> Both inspiration and illumination are ministries of the same Holy Spirit, but this common source does not mean the terms are interchangeable. The key difference between the doctrine of inspiration and the doctrine of illumination is this: inspiration is a *completed* process that guaranteed the truthfulness of the Bible by the Spirit's superintending of the revelation we have recorded in Scripture, whereas illumination is a *continuing* work of the Spirit that guides us into all truth. (John 16:13)[3]

Bonhoeffer's hermeneutical perspective provides support for the need for this multifaceted commitment to the Spirit's work:

3. Heisler, *Spirit-Led Preaching*, 41.

> Every attempt at pneumatological interpretation is a prayer, a plea
> for the Holy Spirit, who alone determines, according to its pleasure,
> the hearing and understanding without which the most spiritual
> exegesis will come to naught. Scriptural understanding, interpre-
> tation, preaching, i.e., the knowledge of God begins and ends with
> the plea: "Veni creator spiritus [Come, Creator Spirit]."[4]

Keeping in tune with the Spirit's leading and wisdom as one prepares to
preach will require a regular expression of the same prayer as the psalmist:
"I am your servant; give me understanding, that I may know your testimonies!" (Psa 119:125, ESV).

Dependence upon the work of the Holy Spirit in the hermeneutical
process does not nullify the importance of the role of understanding the
influence of tradition, culture, and experience in one's approach to any
particular biblical passage. Biblical exegesis and theological reflection are
not done without these influences being involved.[5] This truth has been
illustrated for me recently as the staff and elders in my local church (I serve
as an elder) have been wrestling with the Scriptures as we are seeking a biblical understanding of the role of women in leadership roles in our church,
which honors Scripture and provides guidance.

It is in such situations that we need to listen to the wisdom of the late
John Stott:

> We must come to the biblical text with humble, open, receptive
> spirits. We must be ready for God to break through our cultural
> defenses to challenge and to change us. If we come to Scripture
> with our minds made up and closed, we will never hear the thun-
> derclap of his Word. All we will hear is what we want to hear, the
> soothing echoes of our own cultural prejudice.[6]

It is with this humility and honesty that we acknowledge our fallibility and
the presence of prior influences in our lives (e.g. culture, education, etc.).
As we begin our work of theological reflection in our preparation to preach,
there is an order to follow even though it is an interactive process led
by the Spirit.

---

4. Bonhoeffer, "Pneumatological Interpretation of Scripture," 289.

5. A helpful, fuller discussion of these issues may be found in chapter two of
Clarke, *Pauline Theology.*

6. Stott, *Basic Christian Leadership*, 72.

Primacy of Scripture

While Scripture affirms the necessity of the ongoing work of the Spirit in the illumination of the human mind in the hermeneutical process, it is true that Scripture holds a uniquely authoritative position in the theological reflection activity. The testimony of the prophets and the apostles reveals the necessity of special revelation if we are to understand fully the wisdom and ways of God.[7]

Having done one's work in the text (exegesis, background, etc.), the next step is for the preacher to surrender to the truth of the whole of Scripture. This occurs in the reflection process as the preacher takes time to think through the various contexts of the particular passage: immediate, book, genre, and entire biblical story.

The basic principle at work here is "allow Scripture to interpret Scripture." It is the discipline of biblical theology. The question to be asked is, "Where does this passage and the truths revealed in the text fit in the whole story of redemption?" It involves the work of understanding the whole counsel of God (cf. Acts 20:27).[8]

This beginning principle of the reflection process is described well by Kaiser:

> If we believe there is a coherency and a unifying whole within the sixty-six books of the Bible, then that coherency should be first sought out in the scriptures themselves rather than a grid laid over the text, no matter how helpful that grid may be on other grounds. It is this priority, which is given to that unity and coherence discovered in the Bible itself, that must take precedence over all other theological tasks before we start introducing any confessions or creeds as if they were a shortcut to getting a biblical theology right in the first place.[9]

Beginning at this point in one's reflection upon the text will be an important step in assuring that the message to be preached is faithful to the whole revelation of God as given in Scripture.

---

7. See Isaiah 55:8–9; 2 Timothy 3:16–17.

8. My colleague Robert Smith Jr. defines the whole counsel of God as "that broad concept that unites and ties together every passage of scripture so that it relates to the overall plan and comprehensive purpose of God revealed in the Bible by the Holy Spirit in order to magnify Jesus Christ." Note the Trinitarian scope of the definition.

9. Kaiser and Silva, *Introduction*, 75.

Tradition as a Resource

Now one is ready to bring into the process the historic traditions of the church and one's own particular systematic theological distinctives. There is a need to maintain continuity with historic orthodox church teaching.

Apostles' Creed

The great principles of historic Christian orthodoxy are embedded in this statement of faith and provide guidance for reflection:

I believe in God, the Father almighty, maker of heaven and earth;

And in Jesus Christ his only son our Lord;
Who was conceived by the Holy Ghost,
Born of the Virgin Mary,
Suffered under Pontius Pilate,
Was crucified, dead, and buried.
He descended into hell.
The third day he rose again from the dead.
He ascended into heaven,
And sitteth on the right hand of God the Father almighty.
From thence he shall come to judge the quick and the dead.

I believe in the Holy Ghost,
The holy catholic Church,
The communion of saints,
The forgiveness of sins,
The resurrection of the body,
And the life everlasting.

Amen.

Five Solae

Although not systematically arranged together until a later date, the five *solae* summarize the core beliefs of the sixteenth-century Reformers. They are: *sola scriptura* (by Scripture alone, Matt 4:4), *sola fide* (by faith alone, Gal

2:16), *sola gratia* (by grace alone, Eph 2:8), *solus Christus* (through Christ alone, 1 Tim 2:5), and *soli Deo Gloria* (glory to God alone, 1Cor 10:31).

These five Latin phrases provide another "filter" to use in the process of reflection upon the content of a sermon and in an expanded way upon the broader scope of the preacher's work.

Denominational Heritage

Each particular denominational heritage provides a perspective for viewing a text. In their very helpful book, *How to Read the Bible for All Its Worth*, Gordon Fee and Douglas Stuart provide some great examples in their chapter on Acts concerning how different denominational backgrounds may approach the same text differently.[10]

During the process of reflection, it is helpful to consider the text through one's own denominational bias, but also to consider how other heritages of faith might view the text. Again, the key word for making this a fruitful exercise is "humility."

One of the values of the variety of denominations is that individuals are reached in different ways and different denominations have different strengths. However, each denominational group also has its own unique way of viewing Scripture and none of those is infallible.

Life Experience as Blessing and Curse

When I was a nineteen-year-old Bible college freshman, a professor made a statement in class that made me mad. He said that none of us could fully comprehend the story of the Prodigal Son unless we were a parent. I knew he was wrong! Now, I know he was right!

The experiences of our lives shape our view and understanding of Scripture. The reflective process should take us on a journey inward so that we apply the lessons we have learned through our family experiences, crises, and community of faith as we stay in the text in order to preach to the heart. This will require honesty and transparency.

---

10. Fee and Stuart, *How to Read the Bible*, 107–125.

Family

Our family experience during our early years shapes who we become and how we view life to a considerable degree. For instance, a child with an abusive father will tend toward a much different view of "God as Father" than a child who is raised by a caring, involved father.

Being raised in a strict, legalistic environment can have a large impact on one's view of grace. Indulgent parents can influence a child's sense of entitlement.

In the reflective process, this aspect can help the preacher connect in new ways with the audience. It also can help one avoid living out one's own "stuff" through the sermon. For example, unresolved anger toward a parent can result in preaching that carries a consistent hostile and judgmental tone.

Crises

Experiences of a crisis nature are both painful and instructive. Through them we learn life lessons and through them we will experience growth if we are patient (cf. Jas 1:2–4). Part of that growth will be in how we view specific passages of Scripture. For me, I could not fully comprehend the comfort which God gives during grief until my grandparents were killed in an automobile accident. And I could not deeply comfort others going through grief until I went through that valley of sorrow. Through these experiences we become the "wounded healers" described by Henri Nouwen.

Community of Faith

The community of faith in which one comes to experience the grace of Christ and embrace His forgiveness will have a large impact on the formative years. Teachers, sponsors, and pastors all are crucial in faith development and the perspective with which one approaches all of Scripture. While this may change over time as one matures, it remains as the initial foundation.

All three of these aspects of life experience can be utilized to evaluate their impact upon the focus of the text and the tone of the text as it is presented.

Culture Is Not Neutral

Cultural factors are involved in our study of the background of a particular text and in our personal reflection of our understanding of that text. A good exegete understands that there are several factors involved in grasping the historical context of a passage: geography, political factors, social factors, etc. The same is true for self-understanding in order to practice good reflection.

Geography

For those who have traveled to various regions of the United States or to other countries, there is an awareness of the impact of geography upon how one understands the world. An individual who was raised in the "Bible Belt" culture of the Southern US views the world and the church in a much different way than an individual who spent most of his or her life in the Northeastern states.

My wife and I experienced a time of cultural transition when we moved from Illinois to Alabama. Actually, after nine years, it is still occurring. Customs and expectations are much different.

The differences are more graphic when going from one country to another. When I spent time in southern India at a Christian college, it was a challenging experience as I attempted to teach Scripture to a group of students who had a very different view of the world and had been shaped by their culture. I understood how much my approach to particular passages was conditioned by my own cultural perspective from the United States!

Historical Context

An important companion to geography is historical context. Preachers come from a variety of historical eras, as do their audiences. Several generations are represented each time the preacher presents a message.

When I stand in the pulpit at Beeson Divinity School, I look upon a broad variety of individuals who bring their own prejudices to the communication process out of their particular historical contexts. One African American individual grew up in the South in the 1950s and was not allowed in the public library in her community. One Caucasian person grew up in a wealthy family in the South during the same era and had a black maid who worked for his family. Another individual spent his formative years living in Malaysia as the child of a missionary during the late 1980s.

My own journey took place in a community and in a time when there was strong prejudice against individuals who were not from our faith group. Interdenominational cooperation was nonexistent. In addition, those from other ethnic groups were often ridiculed and viewed as inferior.

One simple illustration of application of these aspects of culture is my own experience of reading Eric Metaxas's book on Bonhoeffer.[11] My understanding of Bonhoeffer's theology and teaching is much richer as I have learned more about his historical and geographical context in Germany in the 1930s and 1940s.

Moving from Exegesis to Communication

Using Tradition, Experience, and Culture as Double Lenses

As the preacher begins to move from exegesis to preparation in order to communicate the truth of a particular biblical passage, his reflection upon tradition, experience, and culture should be utilized as a set of lenses that are viewed through both sides.

The first question to be asked is: "How do tradition, experience, and culture shape my perspective as I seek to understand this text?" An example for me would be my view of 1 Tim 2:8–15 as shaped by my own history in a theologically conservative church and my initial teaching about biblical interpretation from a seminary in the Stone-Campbell heritage. This history would also have an impact on my preaching about marriage from Eph 5:22–33.

The second question to be asked is: "How does this text address tradition, experience, and culture in my current pastoral context?" For instance, when I look at the current practices in my congregation, does this text speak to changes that need to be implemented in the profession or practice of our faith? If so, are there ways to communicate this in a manner that helps the listeners respond rather than react?

As noted previously, the ongoing work of the Holy Spirit is absolutely crucial if this part of the process is to bring new insights when needed or to reinforce current teaching if warranted.

---

11. Metaxas, *Bonhoeffer*.

The Role of Community in Reflection

One of the dangers present in moving from exegesis to communication is to believe that one's own perspective on the text is the same as everyone else's in the faith community. This danger underscores the need to review the exegesis and the sermon itself in the context of other believers. There are two primary ways to accomplish this task.

First, the preacher can schedule a time before each sermon (weekly, or prior to a series) for a review by a small group of other believers who can give him their reflection on his approach to the text(s). This is most beneficial when the group consists of a wide variety of individuals from various life situations and experiences. Some pastors currently maintain the practice of meeting with other pastors to discuss their sermons. While this is helpful, it might be more beneficial to include some lay people in the process.

Second, if the first approach is not reasonable given one's context, the preacher can develop a "mind map" of various individuals in his congregation and review the sermon from their perspectives. For example, how would that older widow in the congregation view this text? Or, how would that recovering alcoholic view it? Or, what does that single mom need to hear from the text? Or, will this speak to the heart of my leaders?

The involvement of a larger community in the theological reflection process does not mean that the preacher will cater to the whims of others, but it does mean that he will gain new perspectives in presenting the text in a manner that speaks to the heart and to the head.

Spirit and Word

Moving from exegesis to communication is one piece of that Spirit-directed process of theological reflection. The preacher will pray earnestly for the illumination which comes from the Holy Spirit during this process, seeking the Spirit's wisdom as he seeks to bring the work of exegesis into the form of the sermon which is intended to reach into the hearts of the people.

"The responsibility of teachers [and preachers] today is to be expositors of the apostolic teaching as recorded in the New Testament [and the Old Testament], faithfully applying it to the contemporary world and making it live for people, transforming them through the anointing of the Holy Spirit."[12]

12. Tidball, *Ministry*, 132.

Preaching to the Heart

The primary aim of this process of theological reflection as part of the preaching task is to develop messages that will communicate on a deeper level, a heart level, with the hearers. Understanding that the Holy Spirit is the one who ultimately brings comfort, conviction, or challenge to a heart, it is the preacher's responsibility to target the heart and not just the head of his hearers.

Where do you begin in the evaluation process *prior* to the preaching of the sermon in order to determine if the heart is the target? I would suggest using the three categories below.

Effect of Our "Fallenness"

The first category is to remember the nature of our human condition. The wording may vary according to one's theological tradition, but the truth remains the same: we are all sinful, fallen creatures. We are all in need of the saving grace of Jesus Christ. And we cannot save ourselves through our works.

Since we are fallen and sinful, there are common needs that we experience. We all need justification and forgiveness of sin. This is only possible through a relationship with Jesus Christ. We enter this relationship through faith in the gospel and relying on the crucified and risen Christ. This means that we must be honest that there is "bad news" which must be proclaimed in order for individuals to sense the need/conviction for the "good news." So, we live with this tension as we preach to the hearts of people while seeking to be faithful to this universal truth.

We are to embrace the biblical truth that our fallenness has separated us from God, ourselves, and others. This reality shapes the actions of unbelievers and continues to be a part of the believer's process of becoming more like Christ. The ultimate reunification of all of these only takes place in Jesus Christ (cf. Eph 1:10). Again, the gospel is our message to speak to the heart of each person in his brokenness and separation from God and others.

Life Stages

The second category is that of utilizing the demands faced by people who are in various life stages. This is one reason it is important to have a variety of ages represented in the group that reviews your sermon plans.

One tool which I have found to be helpful is the chart on family development found in the book by Jack and Judith Balswick *The Family*.[13] They list these life stages as: Premarital, Marital Dyad, Triad, Completed Family, Family with Adolescents, Launching, and Postlaunching.

Obviously, the preacher cannot seek to address every stage in every sermon. However, it is helpful to review these regularly in order to keep some balance in seeking to speak to heart needs.

"Heart Hungers"

The third category provides a general template for considering some basic human needs. There are various ways to articulate these needs. I have found the categories given by Ronald Heifetz and Marty Linsky to be helpful:

1. Power and Control

2. Affirmation and Importance

3. Intimacy and Delight[14]

In the midst of a rapidly changing world with growing chaos, people want some sense of a measure of control in their life. This heart hunger can be met in very dysfunctional ways or in more healthy ways. As the preacher addresses this particular hunger, he can provide a biblical, Christian way of dealing with this need.

The key word in this second area is affirmation. We all want to know that we make a difference to others and that we are appreciated for our contributions. This need proceeds from the brokenness which came through the separation from God, self, and others in the fall. This particular need is met through gospel-centered service to others in order to bring glory to God. At the same time, we all need positive affirmation from others in our lives. Preaching and teaching about the church as the body of Christ is one way to address this heart hunger.

13. Balswick and Balswick, *Family*, 42.
14. Heifetz and Linsky, *Leadership*, 164.

Heifetz and Linsky have a keen insight concerning the third area. They write, "Human beings need intimacy. We need to be touched and held, emotionally and physically. But some of us are vulnerable in the way we experience this need."[15]

This particular heart hunger may be the most dangerous in our twenty-first-century Western world. Many destructive ways to meet this need have been enlarged through the declining sexual standards in our society and the proliferation of Internet pornography. And some of the most obvious examples have been committed by Christian leaders.

Christian preaching has a positive message to proclaim to this heart hunger. This particular need also reinforces the truth to remember that our preaching is in the context of a community. And a Christian community is intended to provide intimacy in a healthy manner with secure boundaries.

Conclusion

Christian preaching is hard work. It is not completed when the text is exegeted. It is not completed when theological reflection is done. It is only finished as the preacher stands to proclaim the Word of God, staying in the text and preaching to the heart, trusting the Holy Spirit to bring his grace to bear upon the preacher and the hearer!

Such proclamation addresses three primary functions of biblical preaching as noted by the great preacher James Earl Massey:

1. Proclamation—initiating the unbeliever into the faith through the gospel

2. Teaching—instructing the believer about the faith through maturation

3. Therapy—inspiring the matured believer to keep the faith (when tough times come) through inspiration[16]

A practiced discipline of "staying in the text and preaching to the heart" by utilizing this process of theological reflection will enable the preacher to assist his hearers in bridging that famous gap between head and heart, and in becoming doers of the Word and not hearers only.

15. Ibid., 176.

16. Massey, *Responsible Pulpit*. Massey's categories have been expanded upon by Robert Smith Jr., professor of preaching at Beeson Divinity School.

9

The Reciprocity of Preaching and Worship

DINELLE FRANKLAND

DR. SACKETT TEASES ME with great regularity about my lack of interest in his craft. He can do this because he knows the opposite is true. I have great respect for preaching and for preachers. The ministry of Dr. Sacket models this observation by John Stott:

> Thus Word and worship belong indissolubly to each other. All worship is an intelligent and loving response to the revelation of God, because it is the adoration of His Name. Therefore acceptable worship is impossible without preaching. For preaching is making known the Name of the Lord, and worship is praising the Name of the Lord made known. Far from being an alien intrusion into worship, the reading and preaching of the Word are actually indispensable to it. The two cannot be divorced. Indeed, it is their unnatural divorce which accounts for the low level of so much contemporary worship. Our worship is poor because our knowledge of God is poor, and our knowledge of God is poor because our preaching is poor. But when the Word of God is expounded in its fullness, and the congregation begins to glimpse the glory of the living God, they bow down in solemn awe and joyful wonder before his throne. It is preaching which accomplishes this, the proclamation of the Word of God in the power of the Spirt of God. That is why preaching is unique and irreplaceable.[1]

1. Stott, *Between Two Worlds*, 82–83.

Worship, however, has had an oddly distant relationship with preaching for most of my lifetime. For many, preaching is the "main event" of Sunday and all else falls subservient to it. For others, the other elements of the Sunday gathering are chosen to enhance the sermon by driving home a particular point. Sadly, many churches see no relationship between the message and the rest of the gathering.

This disconnect is primarily due to the development of the Sunday gathering over time. Early church documents suggest a twofold gathering centered on the sharing of the Word and the celebration of the Lord's Supper. These two foci were surrounded by Scripture reading, praying, singing, and baptisms. Eventually the liturgy became convoluted in such a way that the importance of the sermon was lost. The Reformers rightly sought to bring the Word back to prominence. Over time the necessary reforms resulted in many of the other formative elements of the gathering being lost.

The camp meetings of the American frontier in the early 1800s placed a strong emphasis on evangelism, a valid and vital concern. The liturgical actions that remained naturally began to lean toward the evangelistic camp meeting style, with the altar call as the culmination of the experience. Therefore, the sermon, with a strong evangelistic message, gained a prominent place within the Sunday gathering during this period.[2]

Another component of disconnect is the influence of the Enlightenment. Simply stated, while the premodern world embraced mystery, the Age of Reason valued logic. The sermon lent itself to explanation and "the church became a lecture hall and the minister a moral instructor."[3]

The typical evangelical church of the twentieth century had all of this historical baggage to thank for its worship practices, including a lack of affinity between the sermon and other elements of the gathering. By midcentury, little thought was given to the planning of the gathering until it was suggested that the components of the Sunday hour ought to be based upon one theme, usually the theme of the sermon. While this innovation brought attention to the need for planning and synergy, the sermon remained at the center of the gathering.

Finally, the praise and worship movement, in an attempt to keep pace with culture, has produced a style that is often musically driven. The roots of this movement are nebulous and difficult to pinpoint, but it has

2. Butzu and Shields, *Generations of Praise,* 293–95.
3. Senn, *Christian Worship,* 46.

nevertheless affected many evangelical churches of today. The emphasis is on freedom, remaining contemporary, and meeting felt needs.

This historical overview is an attempt to clarify the building blocks that have contributed to the confusion surrounding the relationship between the sermon and other worship practices. An unfortunate consequence of this misconception is that preachers and worship leaders have failed to be allies in planning the Sunday gathering. This essay seeks to find collaborative ground to unite them in a common purpose. Three underlying worship principles lay the groundwork for this discussion.

First, biblical worship is not relegated to Sunday. While the corporate nature of worship is clearly seen as important throughout the biblical narrative, the emphasis is always on the heart of the worshiper. The Pentateuch stresses acts of obedience, faithfulness, and holiness as necessary for true worship (Exod 19:5–6; Lev 19:2; Deut 10:12–13). The psalmists model praise, thanksgiving, confession, and lament as integral to a relationship with Almighty God (Pss 103; 51; 56). The prophets point to the breaking of the covenant and false worship as detestable in the eyes of God (Isa 1:10–15a; Amos 5:21–25; Mic 6:6–8).

Jesus, in his encounter with the Samaritan woman, shifted the conversation from the place, or form, of worship, to the nature of worship (John 4:21–24). The newly formed church gathered to hear the Word of God, spoken and preached, as well as to sing, pray, and celebrate the Lord's Supper; they also shared the deep fellowship made possible only through the work of the Holy Spirit. The Epistles reframe the expectations of the old covenant in light of the work of Jesus. The exhortation of Paul toward spiritual worship used language that his readers would have recognized from their Jewish past: "Offer your bodies as living sacrifices, holy and pleasing to God" (Rom 12:1). Worship permeates all of life.

The second principle is that worship is, fundamentally, a response to God. Thomas Long reminds the gathered community where the emphasis should be placed.

> It is important to keep reminding ourselves of the strange truth that, odd as it may sound, worship is best measured not by how popular, inspirational, beautiful, educational, musically rich, poetic, or exciting it is. Good worship often is all of these things; indeed true worship has its own beauty, takes dramatic shape, summons the best of language, music, and the arts, and powerfully lifts the human heart. But if we make any of these qualities the goal or primary standard of worship we have badly missed the point. In

essence, worship is what happens when people become aware that they are in the presence of the living God.[4]

In Scripture, worship is not so much defined as described. The Old Testament describes the worship of Israel as being centered upon the work of God to redeem his chosen people. The Exodus story permeated communal gatherings. For example, Deuteronomy 26, which pictures a future gathering of worship, outlines a succinct version of the redemptive process, from slavery to the promised land. God required his children to repeat this story so that it would never be forgotten.[5]

Israel was also instructed to reenact the redemptive process in the form of the Passover meal and other festivals. These gatherings were designed to bring the past into the present in a powerful and palpable manner. The Passover meal retold the Exodus event not just with words, but with actions enlivened by touch, taste, and smell. Because of this consistent and powerful emphasis, redemption remains at the heart of Jewish worship today. The story is seen not as *a* story, but as *our* story. It is not relegated to the distant past, but is valued and claimed for both the present and the future.

It is not difficult to see how the earliest Christians would have reimagined their gatherings around the story that had been theirs for generations. Worship, as they knew it, was centered upon the God who had brought them out of slavery. The grand and miraculous redemptive plan of the Exodus was supplanted by the work of Jesus Christ, requiring an adjustment in the telling of the story.

The New Testament does not prescribe any particular formula for the activities of the gathered community. The first gatherings of Christians drew largely from synagogue practices and were filled with prayer, Scripture, preaching, and singing that remembered the whole history of salvation. In the Lord's Supper and baptism the work of Jesus to redeem a fallen world was remembered and reenacted. The recorded sermons are evangelistic in purpose and in venue; as such they are powerful rehearsals of the gospel story.[6] The Epistles, meant to be read in the assembly, are filled with the Christian's responsibility to know, teach, and live the good

---

4. Long, *Beyond the Worship Wars*, 18.

5. See also Exod 15:1–18; Deut 6:1–25; Psa 77.

6. Notably, Peter's sermon on Pentecost (Acts 2:14–41) and Paul's sermon in Athens (Acts 17:22–31).

news. Today our primary corporate response is still to remember, retell, and reenact the gospel story.[7]

The third principle is that worship as practiced by the assembly is formative. For several hundred years, gatherings have been planned with the end goal of education. The notion that the reason for gathering as a community is primarily didactic ignores both the biblical understanding of worship and hundreds of years of church history. Bryan Chapell notes, "The negative impact of turning the sanctuary into the lecture hall is training believers to become merely reflective about the gospel in worship and tempting them to believe that right worship is simply about right thought. As a consequence, the worship focus becomes study, accumulating doctrinal knowledge, evaluating the Sermon, and critiquing the doctrinally imprecise."[8]

While a major objective on Sunday is for the congregation to learn from the message, there is also the intent that they are moved to grow in Christ, to spread the gospel, to love one another, and to be responsible Christians in a complicated world. The onus of this kind of intense formation does not rest on the sermon alone, but may also be accomplished through singing, praying, Scripture reading, Communion celebrations, and baptisms, all of which have been a part of the corporate worship of the church since its beginning.

Furthermore, the gathered community finds strength through common ground and common practice. By doing so, it sets an example for lost souls seeking comfort, answers, meaning, and genuine care. The Sunday gathering is a place of hospitality, welcome to all.

Fred Craddock aptly describes the nature of the gathering:

> An assembly of believers gathers to worship; that is, to narrate in word, act, and song the community's memories and hopes, glorifying God who redeems, enables, and sanctifies. These have come to renew their vision, to hear and to speak the grand metaphors about how life and the world should be, and to do so with such trust in God that past tenses will be used as though these things were already true. And in this time and place of prayer and praise we will preach.[9]

When viewed in this light, the sermon and worship may be seen as having a reciprocal relationship. Reciprocity is a mutual exchange of privileges, action,

7. See Frankland, *His Story*, 58–77.

8. Chapell, *Christ Centered Preaching*, 67.

9. Craddock, *Preaching*, 41–42.

or influence. In this case, the action being shared is that of responding to the gospel story. The activities that make up a gathering on any given Sunday are woven together to create the tapestry of that story. Reciprocity is different from the "thematic" services of old, in which the sermon dictates each element. Instead, the theme is the work of Jesus Christ to save a lost and dying world. Each week, the people of God see themselves in that story, from creation to consummation. Every element, from the first hello to the final amen, has its place. The following directives are offered to assist preachers and worship leaders in developing an awareness of their shared responsibility.

Preaching *Is* Worship

Much confusion about worship stems from faulty nomenclature. Often, the gathering of believers on Sunday is named worship, which belies the biblical picture described above. After the faithful have gathered, the singing is called worship, which in turn is expected to serve as a preparatory exercise for the sermon. This representation of worship leads the congregation to view the sermon as the primary focus.

The antidote for this label is a return to the basic definition of worship. When the preacher and congregation recognize that the sermon is, in and of itself, a response to God, it becomes a sacrificial gift. Frank Cairns, while admitting this view may not be popular, exhorts preachers:

> Gentlemen, if you are ever to serve God by your preaching, you have got to make up your mind as to whether it has or has not the right to be regarded as an essential part of the worship of God; you must have a clear idea as to whether your preaching is for you an act of worship—an offering to God which you can make with a clear conscience, and a wholehearted devotion, and a humble faith, or whether it is something which—be it either cheap or tawdry, or manifesting both erudition and literary skill—could not be regarded as possessing the authority of the Word of God or any Divine Sanction whatsoever, and which might as well be tied in a napkin and buried in the earth for all the value it has for the purpose of bringing the human soul face-to-face with God.[10]

An offering of this sort is bathed in prayer and wholly dependent upon the guidance of the Holy Spirit to impact souls. It is not selfish, and does not demand the spotlight; nor does it dismiss the notion that God can work in

10. Cairns, *Prophet of the Heart*, 56–57.

a myriad of ways. It will be knit together with other acts of worship to form a carefully woven fabric that draws people into the great redemptive story.

Chris Erdman describes a season of his ministry when he began to seek positive reinforcement from his parishioners based upon his entertaining illustrations:

> I began to realize that people loved the stories I told, the illustrations that populated my well-crafted sermons, but showed little evidence that they were growing in their love for the Story. They were increasingly dependent on my words, but not on the Word. That troubled me. I began to long for someone to come out of worship, shake my hand, and say, "Preacher, that text came alive for me today, and I don't think I'll be able to shake it off. It's disturbed something inside of me, and it may well take the week to make some kind of sense about what it wants to do to us as a church."[11]

Erdman reached the conclusion that he had to return the emphasis to the Bible, not the preacher. When he did, he began to get the kind of comments that showed that members of his congregation were finding their place in the gospel story.

The sermon will not be an act of worship unless the preacher is a whole-life worshiper. Warren Wiersbe admonishes, "A message from God is the living consequence of a vital meeting with God during which you worshiped Him and permitted His truth to set fire to your soul. When the minister's study turns into a sanctuary, a Holy of Holies, then something transforming will happen as the Word of God is proclaimed."[12]

While preaching is an act of worship for the preacher, the congregation worships by listening. Often, other responses are seen as active, while the sermon is considered a passive requirement for the congregation. Wiersbe contends, "When the man or woman in the pew opens the Bible and pays attention to the preacher, there is no jarring note, nor is it necessary to 'shift gears' either mentally or emotionally. From the beginning of the service to the end, our eyes are open to God's glory and our ears to God's truth. There are no 'preliminaries' to be 'gotten out of the way.'"[13]

11. Erdman, *Countdown to Sunday*, 111–12.

12. Wiersbe, *Real Worship*, 127.

13. Ibid.,126–27.

Preaching is Proclamation, but
Not the Only Proclamation

C. Welton Gaddy insists that "worship *is* proclamation—all of it, at least implicitly. Proclamation is a part of worship—a major part of it explicitly. *In* worship and *through* worship, the great truths of the Bible are proclaimed by words and actions."[14] Of course, preaching "is unique in its ability to challenge, encourage, and to guide people regarding their faith. Preaching not only conveys the gospel, it participates in the gospel."[15] The Holy Spirit, however, may also work through other elements within the gathering to proclaim the gospel and evoke response.

Ken Read suggests that worship leaders have a certain prophetic role, perhaps as "a church musician with a preacher's heart."[16] He notes that those who plan the Sunday gathering are putting a kind of sermon together, most often with the words of others in the form of songs, Scripture readings, dramas, etc. Therefore, he encourages worship leaders, "God may have called you to be a preacher, but not in the traditional sense of delivering sermons."[17]

One of the primary vehicles for this heightened understanding of proclamation is singing. Brian Wren asks the important question, "What if strong congregational singing not only encourages and inspires, but helps form our spirituality and shape our theology?"[18] The answer, of course, is that it does just that, for good or for ill. Music, a generous gift from God, may provide an avenue to touch souls with his love, to teach minds his truth, and to empower hearts with the his strength. It is erroneous to suggest that this potency is in the music itself; on the other hand, it is dangerous to ignore the power that poorly chosen music may have upon the children of God who absorb it over and over.

Another means of proclamation is the reading of Scripture aloud. Once a strong component of worship gatherings, it has lost its significance as a major place to hear the voice of God. Robert Webber argues for returning Scripture, at least in part, to the congregation. He says, "I want to feel and experience the whole drama of redemption in such a way that the story

14. Gaddy, *Gift of Worship*, 132.

15. Ibid., 141.

16. Read, *Created to Worship*, 202.

17. Ibid., 202–03.

18. Wren, *Praying Twice*, 47.

of my own pilgrimage is gathered up into that drama and given meaning. In this way, the Word is not merely words, but life. It creates the body of Christ and reaffirms faith within me."[19] The sermon is not the only means of hearing and interacting with the Word. The thoughtful use of Scripture reading helps move the story along, filling in significant parts that might be missed, while penetrating the soul.

The Lord's Supper and the celebration of baptisms also play important roles in proclaiming the history and grandeur of God's redemptive plan. These corporate moments have the distinction of being enacted parables, proclamations that are visible and interactive. For much of recent history, they have been diminished in importance to the point that they are in danger of losing their efficacy. [20] Sharing the bread and cup may be individual rather than communal, somber rather than celebratory, divisive rather than unified. Baptisms may also be individualized, missing an opportunity for the community to reaffirm the unity of the Spirit. Rarely do worship leaders or preachers recognize the importance of surrounding these celebrations with meaningful, appropriate words and actions. Yet both have a place of supreme importance in the recital of the gospel.

Careful planning enables an experience that seamlessly connects the parts of the gathering to form a unified whole. Bob Kauflin observes that in this kind of gathering we are "proclaiming God's truth with our lives. We're doing more than emoting or having a 'worship experience.' We're declaring why God is so great, what he has accomplished, and all that he has promised. We all need to be reminded, and proclamation helps us remember."[21]

Planning Requires a Relationship

Rehearsing the gospel story with consistency and vibrancy requires a relationship between the preacher and those charged with developing the other elements of the gathering. The elements flow together—they tell a story and create a conversation. This story has more depth and breadth if the conversation begins well before Sunday. If there is no communication between the preacher and the designer of the gathering, at best the parts are disconnected; at worst, they are contradictory. Rochelle Stackhouse suggests, "If both music and preaching are embodied Words—proclamations

19. Webber, *Worship is a Verb,* 95.

20. Frankland, *His Story,* 69–72, 124–126.

21. Kauflin, *Worship Matters,* 129.

of the gospel—then both preachers and musicians need to make sure that the proclamation that comes in all acts of the drama of worship is consistent and mutually supportive."[22]

Mutual support is more than offering a sermon text and a time limit (although many worship leaders would be pleased to have even that amount of information). Rather, the elements come together in the same way a sermon does, with prayer, study, and humility. A gathering has a beginning and a conclusion; it fits the pieces of the story together like a finely wrought musical composition; it holds in great regard the members of the particular body for which it has been conceived. Such mutual support assures that one gift, particularly the preaching gift, is not elevated above others.

Some worship leaders plan services from unhealthy starting points. They believe that music, or perhaps some other element of the gathering, deserves the most attention. Others have not grasped the concept that their music is an offering, not a performance, and do not have a rich worship life. But often the worship leader, who has been given the influential task of speaking theologically, has a shallow and disconnected relationship with the preacher, who should be a positive, forceful influence.

Such a reality need not be the case. A former student was required to meet regularly with his senior minister in order to fulfill the requirements of an internship. When asked to evaluate the process, he stated that he did not want the internship to end because it was so fulfilling to sit down regularly with his preacher and discuss worship. A supportive relationship ought to be the norm, not the exception.

Mutual Respect Is Essential

The Holy Spirit works through meetings, discussions, and relationships, as well as in the hour on Sunday. It is crucial that the preacher and the planning team have developed a strong theology of worship, along with continuous conversations about the nature of worship. When disagreements about the use of particular elements arise, and they will, these respectful deliberations will result in the ability to speak as one on the issue.

In order for the elements of the Sunday gathering to be reciprocal in nature, there must be an appreciation for the skills necessary to accomplish an integrated whole. A mutual accountability toward biblical fidelity is essential. A good worship planner is also an interpreter, not only of Scripture,

22. Stackhouse, "Music, Proclamation and Praise," 91.

but also of lyrics and music. For this reason, preachers should encourage those charged with the content of the gathering to give a portion of their training to in-depth biblical study alongside the necessary development of musical skills. In turn, preachers need to study worship, both through a biblical lens and from the perspective of history.

Worship leaders are also required to have a watchful eye on culture, in particular the culture that is derived from the congregation's own unique context. Attention to culture is not about likes and dislikes or gimmicks the church across town has used with apparent success. It is not about following the whims of pop culture. Rather, it is about spending time with the group of believers that walk through your doors every Sunday, in order to hear their real needs, hurts, and joys. The culture of a community is discovered by being a part of that community. Preachers and worship leaders can and should explore this together.

The Preacher Is an Example

The congregation looks up to the preacher. They will follow cues about full participation, appreciation for the worship team, and giving attention to the importance of all elements. Walking in after the gathering has already begun, shuffling through sermon notes during the singing, and being less than thoroughly engaged until the sermon begins does an injustice, not only to God, but to the rest of the team and the preacher's own worship life.

Worship leaders have the responsibility to shepherd their team toward full participation as well. One helpful exercise is to share with the team, perhaps at rehearsal, how the story is being told and to pray together for the message to be grasped in incomprehensible ways. It is easy for the worship team to disappear behind the stage during the sermon, but they should be a visible presence as supporters and active listeners of the entire proclamation, not just their part in it.

The Practical Expectation

You may have begun this chapter, either as a preacher, worship leader, or congregational participant, hoping to come away with specific, practical suggestions for planning a Sunday gathering. There is no single formula for planning that is proper and fitting for every body of believers. There are many good books that will help with ideas and resources for developing innovative and thoughtful gatherings.[23]

Planning and deliberations begin with the sermon text and topic. When the preacher and the worship planner have done their homework, have agreed upon a theology of worship, have carefully considered the culture of the body, and have respect for each other's skills, the planning table is supportive and creative. The question is asked, "What part of the gospel does the sermon tell?" The task becomes, "What can we do to tell the rest of the story?"

The challenge for all involved is to work together to tell the gospel story to the specific group of people that God places under your care Sunday after Sunday. Tell it with excitement, tell it with hope, tell it in its entirety; tell it to the lost and to the saved, tell it to the young and to the old, tell it to the rich and to the poor; tell it with all of your heart, soul, and strength. Most importantly, tell it together.

---

23. See Cherry, *Worship Architect*; Yoder et al., *Preparing Sunday Dinner*; and Beach, *An Hour On Sunday*.

10

The Preacher as the Lead Student

J. K. JONES

THE PREACHER WHO STUDIES is wise. The preacher who has a congregation that expects him to study is blessed. In tribute to my dear friend and trusted colleague, Chuck Sackett, I would like to devote a chapter to the preacher as the lead student. It was, for a season, my enormous honor and high privilege to partner with him in teaching the art and science of preaching at Lincoln Christian University in Lincoln, Illinois. I believe that Dr. Chuck Sackett is an exemplary model of what I want to talk about in this essay. He would agree with Donald Whitney's description of study. Whitney writes:

> If reading the Bible can be compared to cruising the width of a clear, sparkling lake in a motorboat, studying the Bible is like slowly crossing the same lake in a glass-bottomed boat. The motorboat crossing provides an overview of the lake and a swift, passing view of its depths. The glass-bottomed boat of study, however, takes you beneath the surface of Scripture for an unhurried look of clarity and detail that's normally missed by those who simply read the text.[1]

Reading the Bible widens our view of God's good news, but study deepens that view. If there ever was a time where church and culture needed a preacher with depth, it is now. The shallowness of our age and the lack of deep Scriptural roots makes this an unfortunate reality.

1. Whitney, *Spiritual Disciplines*, 31.

There are two passages from Scripture, one Old Testament and one New Testament, that I would like to explore as foundational for the preacher as a lead student. Over the years I have tried to stay tethered to these two supreme biblical texts. The first is Ezra 7:10 and the second is 2 Tim 2:15. Before I reflect on them, let me step aside and allow some of Chuck's favorite voices to shape our discussion. He listened and learned from other preachers, especially their lives of study.

Dr. Sackett was always grateful to his heritage without being enslaved to it. First, hear the words of a Stone-Campbell Movement teacher of preachers, Dr. Alger Fitch (1919–2014), in his classic, *What the Bible Says about Preaching*. Fitch declares:

> Thinking precedes speaking or regret follows it. Prior to the commission, "go preach," were the many occasions when Christ took "the Twelve aside . . . " Quiet occasions without distraction were necessary for clarity of message. . . . Let your ears and eyes get their full-week's exercise before your mouth begins its Sunday morning jog. Hours of serious reflection will enhance the minutes of pulpit projection. . . . The people of the world do not trust an amateur to play surgeon, when a critical and life-threatening operation faces them. The people in the pew want no half-hearted person dealing with their eternal souls. They want a preacher who manifests evidence that he is "God . . . approved" and a "workman who does not need to be ashamed."[2]

Fred Craddock's voice is one that Chuck and I have admired deeply. His words are acutely appropriate to this essay. Few say it better than he does. Dr. Craddock advises:

> When the life of study is confined to "getting up sermons," very likely those sermons are undernourished. They are the sermons of a preacher with the mind of a consumer, not a producer, the mind that looks upon life in and out of books in terms of usefulness for next Sunday. . . . Studying only for the next sermon is very much like clearing out of the wilderness a small garden patch, only to discover the next week that the wilderness has again taken over. . . . Time spent in study is never *getting away* from daily work but *getting into* daily work. The hours of study bear directly and immediately on who the minister is and the minister's influence by word and action. It is in the study that so much of the minister's formation of character and faith takes place. There are many terms

2. Fitch, *What the Bible Says About Preaching*, 86–87.

to describe this activity. Study is an act of obedience. . . . What minister has not experienced a desk becoming an altar? It is a time of pastoral work; the entire congregation will benefit from the fruit of this labor. . . . Study is getting a second and third opinion before diagnosis and treatment. . . . Study is a homiletical act: the confidence born of study . . . releases the powers of communication.[3]

There are at least two additional voices that Chuck often quoted when challenging students to a life of study. Both Dr. Haddon Robinson and the late John Stott regularly made their way into some part of our preaching classes. Let their words challenge us again. Robinson says:

If people can be exposed to an understanding of the Scriptures on a regular basis, then they do not need arguments about the veracity of Scripture.[4]

Stott writes:

You and I have to accept the discipline of thinking ourselves back into the situation of the biblical authors—their history, geography, culture, and language. If we neglect this task or if we do it in a half-hearted or slovenly way, it is inexcusable. It expresses contempt for the way in which God chose to speak to the world.[5]

Chuck Sackett is an incarnational example of a professor and preacher who models what it means to be an ongoing learner and an apprentice to Jesus Christ. One of the ingredients that I have most valued about our friendship is the way in which his faithful life of study has blessed mine. He continually seeks out the best resources. I add this quotation from Dr. Abraham Kuruvilla, whose work in *Privilege the Text* has recently received much acclaim. It is a fresh and eloquent reminder of the challenge of study. Dr. Kuruvilla states:

The lot of the homiletician is not easy: each week, this intrepid soul has to negotiate the formidable passage from ancient text to modern audience to expound, with authority and relevance, a specific biblical passage for the faithful. The goal of this work is to create a bridge spanning those waters, by employing with profit concepts derived from hermeneutics and theology. . . . Preaching is not only the interpretation of an authoritative biblical text but

3. Craddock, *Preaching*, 69–71.

4. Robinson, "Convictions," 23–24.

5. Stott, "Definition," 26.

also the relevant communication of a God-given message to real people living real lives with a real need for that message.[6]

I will now explore the two passages mentioned above, beginning with Ezra 7:10. Ezra is a superlative model for mature ministry and a life committed to study. Ezra 7 reminds us that this priest's lineage went back to Aaron (7:5). Somewhere around 458 BC, fifty-seven years after Zerubbabel's temple rebuild was completed and dedicated, this scribe, born in captivity, "skilled in the Law of Moses," traveled four months and nine-hundred miles, finally arriving in Jerusalem. Extraordinary! In the immediate context of Ezra 7:10 "scribe" shows up three different times (7:6, 11, 12). It is the defining term in the parallel text of Nehemiah (8:1, 4, 9, 13; 12:26, 36).

A scribe in the ancient Near East was responsible for the reproduction of biblical texts.[7] The training to become a scribe was tedious and time-consuming.[8] What should be noted is that Ezra the scribe was selected by King Artaxerxes and commissioned "to make specific inquiries about Judah and Jerusalem according to the Law of your God . . . and also to carry the silver and gold that the king and his counselors have freely offered to the God of Israel, whose dwelling is in Jerusalem. . . . Whatever Ezra the priest, the scribe of the Law of the God of heaven, requires of you, let it be done with all diligence" (7:14–15, 21, ESV). Scribe is the term applied to someone who not only is able to copy manuscripts, but is a teacher skilled in explaining the law. The Hebrew term *sōpēr* was used for someone "well-versed" in tracking details. Examples outside of Scripture would include military commanders and mathematicians. The excellent *IVP Bible Background Commentary: Old Testament* states:

> As a scribe, Ezra was possibly a member of the Persian bureaucracy. It was a common practice for ancient Near Eastern governments to employ persons trained not only as a secretaries or clerks, but as diplomats and lawyers. These individuals were used to interpret documents from subject and allied peoples. They were also sent on investigative missions to aid the king and his advisors in making decisions. . . . Scribes would have been trained in reading of the various languages in use at the time, in the production of texts . . . in the knowledge of traditional literature . . . and in the

---

6. Kuruvilla, *Privilege the Text*, 19–20.

7. *Zondervan Encyclopedia of the Bible*, s.v. "Scribe, Scribes."

8. This essay will not tackle the contemporary attack on the authenticity of the letter or the historicity of the man.

interpretation of literature. . . . Scribes in Israel were, therefore, experts in the Law of Moses. One of their primary duties was to study the Scripture. They became paramount in Jewish life in the postexilic period.[98]

What, then, can Ezra the scribe teach us about the preacher as the lead student? Ezra 7:10 says, "For Ezra had set his heart to study the Law of the LORD, and to do it and to teach his statutes and rules in Israel." Four characteristics are noteworthy. First, Ezra had *set his heart*; the Hebrew word is *kûn*. Translations of the word vary. The NIV inserts the word "devoted." The NLT uses the word "determined." The KJV selects "prepared" as the translation of choice. It would be proper to translate "set" as "make firm," "establish," or "resolve." Notice that Ezra specifically "set his heart." "Heart" renders the terms used some 1,014 times throughout the Old and New Testaments. "Heart" is most likely a reference to the inner life of a person. It is the real person, the point of contact with God, the deep core of a human being, or the mission control center of all that we are. The Bible first mentions it in Gen 6:5–6, where Scripture declares that the thoughts of man's *heart* were only evil continually. The Genesis writer reveals that "the LORD regretted that he had made man on the earth, and it grieved him to his *heart*." Robert Saucy, in his superb work *Minding the Heart*, offers this insightful observation:

> The Bible's teaching that the heart is the real person—and the source and director of all personal activities—surely means that *the care of our heart is to be the supreme task of our life*. The heart deserves to be guarded "more than any treasure," for it is our treasure of greatest value—our own self (see Mark 8:36–37). What we bring into it, what we allow to slip out from it, what we expel from it—all determine who we are, the direction of our life's journey, and finally, our ultimate destiny.[10]

Ezra, like the proverb says, had kept his heart with "all vigilance" (Prov 4:23). When a preacher sets his heart to lead the way in study, application, and instruction, then the results bear much fruit.

No doubt God leads the way in our transformation as lead learners, but he also invites us into the change process by cooperating with his purposes. In setting our heart as Ezra did, we guard it, renew it, keep it clean, direct it toward God, toward his Word, toward his wisdom, and toward

9. Walton *et al.*, *IVPBBCOT*, 468, 478.

10. Saucy, *Minding the Heart*, 46.

his rule and reign. Sometimes in my own study or in my morning "Tent o Meeting" I will light a candle as a reminder that I have set my heart to seek the God who seeks me, to love the God that loves me, and to know the God that knows me. In the early years of my teaching and preaching, I gave little attention to this vital step of preparation for usefulness in the kingdom. So, let me ask the reader, "Are you fixing your heart every day toward being the lead student in your area of influence?"

The second characteristic that marked Ezra, and must mark all preachers as the lead student as well, is *study*. Ezra set his heart to study. *Dāraš* is the word for study in this text. It means to seek something with the greatest of care. Study provides a picture of someone inquiring and searching with due diligence, in this case, the Word of God. Seth Wilson, long-time Academic Dean of Ozark Christian College in Joplin, Missouri, and now with the Lord, once listed twelve reasons why it was paramount that we study the Bible. His reasons include:

1. To receive the light of truth that God has given and escape the darkness of ignorance which engulfs the unbelieving mass of humanity (Eph 4:17–24; Rom 10:1–3).

2. To obtain the life that God gives us in Christ (Heb 4:12; Jas 1:18; John 20:30–31; 1 John 5:9–13).

3. To be renewed and transformed in our minds and hearts. We are cleansed by the words of Christ (John 15:3; Eph 4:22–24; 5:26–27; Rom 12:2).

4. To be filled with the wisdom and understanding which comes from God, which is true to our nature as God made us, and is valid and valuable for all eternity as well as for earthly relationships and responsibilities (Phil 1:9–11; 4:8–9; Col 2:3–10; 3:1–4).

5. To be able to practice the will of God, that we may please Him and glorify Him to whom we owe all love and service; also that we may be in blessed fellowship with our loving and perfect Heavenly Father (Col 1:9–13; 1 John 1:5–9).

6. To strengthen our faith (Rom 10:17; Eph 3:17; 1 Tim 1:3–19; Heb 10:38–39; 11:1–12:2; 1 John 5:4).

7. To be able to give an answer to everyone that asks a reason for the hope that is in us (1 Pet 3:15; 2 Pet 1:16–21).

8. To be admonished and encouraged by the examples of men who lived before us (1 Cor 10:1–12; Rom 15:4; Heb 11).

9. To be real disciples of Jesus. The word translated *disciple* means a learner. Can we maintain our standing as his disciples without being learners of his Word (Matt 28:19; Jas 1:19–22; 2 Pet 1:3–19)?

10. To avoid false teachings and snares of Satan the deceiver (Rom 16:17–18; 2 Cor 11:3, 13–15; 1 Thessalonians 2:3–10; 1 Tim 4:1–7; 2 Tim 2:14–18, 23–26; 3:1–5; Tit 1:10; 3:9–11).

11. To continue in his Word by which we know the truth and are made free (John 8:31–32; 1 John 5:20; 2 John 9).

12. To let his Word abide in us by which he promises great privileges of prayer (John 15:7), and by which we received the power to bear fruit and to have the full joy of abiding in his love (John 15:3–15).[11]

Brother Wilson was often heard bemoaning the condition of so many churches that were being starved by preachers whose sermons were not nourishing, lacked real Bible study, and were unable to fill the minds of those listeners with the life-giving Word of God. If Ezra wrote Psalm 119, as some advocate, I am reminded how that chapter in scripture is an intense reminder of the Bible's supremacy.[12] It is worthy of study.

A number of years ago, I journeyed with my oldest daughter to Papua New Guinea. Among our many experiences, one will always stand out in my memory. We were privileged to talk with a single woman, a Wycliffe Bible translator from Finland. She had devoted twenty-five years to loving a specific people group. She had researched, learned, mastered, and finally translated their language in order to give them the Word of God in their own heart words. She handed me, with some emotion, her completed manuscript. "This is my life's work," she said. I cried. What else could I do? A life of study is a sacred offering. I was in the midst of greatness. Congregations all over the world are longing for a preacher who will, like Ezra, "set his heart to study." Only preachers that can feed others out of their abundant storehouses, can address the spiritual famine in our day. Do you regularly "eat" from the pages of Scripture? The preacher cannot give away what he has not taken in. Study.

11. Wilson and Gardner, *Learning From God's Word*, 11–12.

12. Koch, "Who Wrote Psa 119?," http://www.the119project.com/#!who-wrote-Psa-119/c9z7.

The third characteristic of Ezra the Scribe that must be ours is *do*. Keep the flow of the verse in mind. He set his heart to study and *do* what he had learned. In other words, Ezra "lived it out." Ezra sounds like James. He was a doer of the Word. The Hebrew word *'āśāh* often describes an ethical obligation. It is the exact term that is used of faithfulness in "keeping" the Passover. Theoretical practice is unacceptable. Yoda was correct: "Do or do not. There is no try." So, are we truly "living out" the Book? Call it obedience. Call it action. Call it practice. Just do it. That's what preachers who are lead students look like. They are doers.

The fourth and final characteristic of Ezra is *teach*. *Lāmad* shows up eighty-seven times in the Old Testament and is one of twelve terms used for teaching or training. Ezra 7:10 describes this priest and scribe as continually teaching what he set his heart to study and do. This was not a one-time event. Ezra kept on teaching. *Teach* is the very term that gets inserted into the magnificent elevation of the Word of God in Psa 119:12, 26, 64, 66, 68, 108, 124, 135, and 171. The part that speaks most deeply to my preacher's heart and the one that I think most resonates in the soul of my friend, Chuck Sackett, is that this word actually incorporates both the learning and teaching elements. Derek Kidner speaks to these elements. He writes of Ezra:

> He is a model reformer in that what he taught he had first lived, and what he lived he had first made sure of in the Scriptures. With study, conduct and teaching put deliberately in this right order, each of these was able to function properly at its best: study was saved from unreality, conduct from uncertainty, and teaching from insincerity and shallowness.[13]

In other words, when we speak of making disciples based on Matthew 28:18–20, we are actually tethered to this Old Testament word. Ezra intended to "make apprentices to God" before the Great Commission existed. Preachers of every stripe should give pause to this immensely important question: Am I giving the Word away in order to craft and train "ongoing learners" in the Jesus way?

I have been blessed to see this very portrait fleshed out in real-life circumstances. Isabel Dittemore might not be a name readily recognized in most circles. In my house she is a heroine of faith. Her story is described in that enchanting book *He Leadeth Me*.[14] Isabelle unfolds the narrative

13. Kidner, *Ezra & Nehemiah*, 62.

14. Dittemore, *He Leadeth Me*, 17.

of her forty years of Christian service in Asia. Numerous experiences of suffering and pain could have brought her service to an end. At one point, she fell and nearly tore her arm off. One of her children, baby Jonathan, suffocated to death at the tender age of three months. Warren, her husband of only a few years, died of typhus. Like so many, she also fled China in 1949 when the Communists came to power. Most of us would have been crippled by any one of those challenges. Isabel pressed on, even enduring an emotional and physical breakdown. Years later, some time in the early 1990s, our family was worshiping at College Heights Christian Church in Joplin, Missouri. My children noticed this elderly woman sitting up front dressed with great color and fashion. They wondered who she was. I told them it was none other than Isabel Dittemore, the missionary. They didn't believe me, so after worship that morning I took them to meet her. That conversation marked their lives. So much was shared, but one defining moment will always stand out in their memories. Isabel pulled out her false teeth and asked my daughters, "What are you willing to do for Jesus?" Knowing that her teeth were a constant problem, she had them pulled so that they would not get in the way of her setting her heart to study, do, and teach people about Jesus in China!

"For Ezra had *set* his heart to *study* the Law of the LORD, and to *do* it and to *teach* his statutes and rules in Israel." That's the Old Testament view of the preacher as lead student. Now we come to the New Testament. 2 Timothy 2:15 declares, "Do your best to present yourself to God as one approved, a worker who has no need to be ashamed, rightly handling the word of truth." Let's recall that Paul had assigned Timothy to minister in Ephesus, the center for Artemis/Diana worship, where religion and sex were routinely intertwined. He wrote these moving words sometime in the mid-to-late 60s CE from the Mamertine Dungeon in Rome, located under the city's main sewer line. In that dark and dirty cell the Holy Spirit lit in the heart of the apostle words that can ignite the preacher as the lead student. Paul's admonition was and is a simple one. All of us who take on the primary responsibility as Word bearers are to be eager, zealous, diligent, and make maximum haste to "rightly handle" the Scriptures.

Orthotomeō is the Greek word for "rightly handling" the word of truth. Literally, the word means "to cut rightly" or straight. This imagery conjures up four possible pictures. First, Paul might have in mind a farmer who has the ability to plant his crops in straight rows. We can recall that Paul even uses this imagery back in 2 Timothy 2:6, where he describes a hard-working farmer. Second, Paul might have in mind a mason or bricklayer. A qualified mason would take the extra effort to use a plumb line to be certain that the block or brick being laid was straight and stood the test of time. The third possibility for "rightly handling" might be that of a butcher or meatcutter. This trade would have been common in the Roman Empire. Disreputable butchers might use all kinds of dishonest means to increase the weight and thus the price of a cut of meat. A butcher might offer a poor cut of meat filled with bone and gristle in order to raise his profits. He might even find some way to cheat the scales. Meatcutters who "rightly handled" their task did so with complete integrity. Fourth and finally, Paul might have been referring to a road builder. In Paul's day, the Roman army expertly built thousands of miles of road. A traveler could log on average thirty to fifty miles a day if journeying by horseback or chariot. Like many, I have visited modern Greece and Turkey and marveled at how so much of that ancient Roman road system is still in existence today. A road worker who skillfully laid out a straight thoroughfare that would last for centuries was someone who "rightly handled" his trade.

The preacher as lead student is a servant of the Word who not only "cuts Scripture correctly," but has the ability to stay on the road of good interpretation and not wander off on tangents (note 2:18—"swerved from the truth"). In the immediate context of 2 Timothy 2:15, apparently Hymenaeus and Philetus were examples of men who failed the test and did not "rightly handle" the word of truth. False teachers and teaching infiltrated the life of the early church. One commentator, Ben Witherington, suggests that Paul actually did not have in mind rightly dividing the Scriptures:

> Probably what is meant here is not "rightly dividing the Scriptures," but rather cutting straight to the point in one's preaching, proclaiming the straight stuff, not beating around the bush with esoterica, unlike the false teachers. . . . Timothy is to speak directly and clearly about the words of truth, to get right to the point, or as we might say now, "cut to the chase."[15]

It is difficult to know exactly what Paul meant here, since this is the only occasion in the New Testament where he incorporates *orthotomeō*. Perhaps John Stott said it best. He suggests: "To 'cut it straight' or 'make it a straight path' is to be accurate on the one hand and plain on the other in

---

15. Witherington, *Letters and Homilies*, 336.

our exposition."[16] Cutting Scripture correctly requires the preacher to be the lead student.

Dr. Chuck Sackett is first and foremost my brother in Christ and my trusted friend. I wanted this essay to have the feel of a loving tribute. I recall those moments in class when he would intensely challenge a student's study of the assigned preaching text. All in-class sermons were videotaped, critiqued, and discussed. Holy conversations involving the student's study habits, interpretation, and application followed. Sometimes Chuck would become agitated at the obvious lack of study on the part of the young preaching students. There were some memorable moments when my friend conducted a "come-to-Jesus meeting" by reminding the students that the life, health, and witness of congregations depended a great deal on their being the lead student in their place of ministry. "The hand of God" was on Ezra and Timothy to accomplish all that his grand purpose desired. That same mighty hand is present today. Study and right interpretation are reminders that teaching and preaching is a sacred partnership between the preacher as lead student and the Sovereign King of the Universe.

> Now to him who is able to keep you from stumbling and to present you blameless before the presence of his glory with great joy, to the only God our Savior, through Jesus Christ our Lord, be glory, majesty, dominion, and authority, before all time and now and forever. Amen. (Jude 24–25)

---

16. Stott, *Message of 2 Timothy*, 67.

11

What Do You Do with All This Snow?
Shaping a Sermon in a Multigenerational Context

Brooks Wilson

Snow is falling again in the Midwest—the stomping grounds of Chuck Sackett over these last few decades of his life and ministry. It collects with astonishing speed, piling up on streets and lawns in huge drifts. The landscape is serene and scary. The beauty of the falling white snow contrasts with the blackened slush that automobiles and salt mixtures have caked onto the roads. It's wintertime in Illinois. The question has become, "What do you do with all that snow?"

Sermon Writing as Snowman Building

Sermon writing is like shaping the snow. Just as snow has fallen graciously onto our world without our input or purchase, so too the words of God have fallen in merciful revelation upon us. They pile up around us with increasing speed, demanding our response. Their numerous shapes can be quite intimidating. So what do you do with these sixty-six books of words freshly fallen into our lives?

Some have seen the great power in the revelatory powder, and so they make weapons of them. A snowball aimed true and flung with force can knock someone over. Many a preacher has used the words of God to do the same. Others sense the protective strength of these words, creating walls and fortresses of theology to shield them and their flock from the dangerous world all around. They dig in defensively behind a snow fort, using God's word as a buffer. Still others want nothing more than to play with these words. They frolic in them, making snow angels and snow cones, treating them as no more important than yesterday's plaything. But when it comes to preaching, the best response is to shape God's words into something pertinent and powerful.

The best preaching is like making a snowman. You roll the snow into large, medium and small mounds. You stack and add accoutrement (carrots, coal, coats, and hats). Your imagination is your only obstacle, really. Each part of the process is sacred and playful. Your rolling of the snowballs (reading, study, *lectio divina*), the shaping of the body together (hermeneutics, canonical, and biblical theology), the adding of face elements and clothing (illustration, metaphor, cultural relevance), and the inclusion of hands and feet (application, correlation, next steps) all add together to create something magical. The best sermons allow enough preparation time to shape them again and again. Sometimes you add snow; sometimes you cut it away.

There is nothing so interesting as a snowman standing as a sentinel in a public place. It's truly beautiful. You know it's been carefully crafted. You know there was hard work involved. You know someone paid the price of cold, tingling fingers with winter whipping at their nose. You can tell on first glance whether an individual put it together or a group of people collaborated. You feel joy; you are whisked away by memories of another time; you are transported into another era outside of yourself.

That moment lasts as long as you consider it. Some see it quickly, smile, and move on. Others drink in the image and it changes them. The latter response is what you hope for in a sermon—your transitory snowman moving someone before it melts away in time. Of course, God provides the snow (biblical material), the temperature (preaching environment), and all the conditions for it to stand proud or to melt on Sunday. But oh what a joy it is to be a part of it all!

Snowflakes and Audience Analysis

It has been said that every snowflake is unique and no two snowflakes are alike.[1] Well if that's true, how do you craft something that reflects the beauty of every individual snowflake while creating something that's beautiful for every individual to behold? How do you make law and story, poem and proverb, gospel and genealogy sparkle for every generation in the church—Builders, Boomers, Busters, and Bridgers?[2]

There are as many audiences for sermons as there are unique snowflakes. Every Chuck Sackett course on preaching will hammer home the importance of audience analysis in sermon preparation.[3] The trick is shaping the sermon into something that each generation can appreciate. But the audience in the American church has changed drastically, even since I sat in Dr. Sackett's courses twenty years ago. And they will continue to change.

For instance, Paul Taylor of the Pew Research Center writes that over the next forty years our nation will get "a whole lot older, as is almost every other nation on the planet—the fruits of longer life spans and lower birthrates that are each unprecedented in human history."[4] He summarizes the generational frame that will shape nearly every aspect of our nation's future:

> As a people, we're growing older, more unequal, more diverse, more mixed race, more digitally linked, more tolerant, less married, less fertile, less religious, less mobile, and less confident. Our political and media institutions have become more polarized and partisan; so has the public itself. Our economy is producing

1. David Phillips, the senior climatologist with Environment Canada, has estimated that the number of snowflakes that have fallen on earth over the course of time is ten followed by thirty-four zeros. Charles Knight at the National Center for Atmospheric Research in Boulder, Colorado, estimates there are 10,000,000,000,000,000,000 water molecules in a typical snow crystal. So Mariana Gosnell concludes, "The way they can arrange themselves is almost infinite. . . . But I think experts are in agreement. The likelihood of two (snowflakes) being identical is next to impossible." See the article by Roach, "'No Two Snowflakes the Same,'" http://news.nationalgeographic.com/news/2007/02/070213-snowflake_2.html.

2. There are numerous nomenclatures used for the generations. Gary McIntosh names them in alliteration (a preacher's best friend?!) in McIntosh, *One Church*, 7. For the rest of this chapter, however, I'll use what are arguably the most common names today: Builders, Baby Boomers, Generation X, and Millennials.

3. While the names of Dr. Sackett's preaching courses have changed, the books he assigned have made a lasting point on this topic. See Loscalzo, *Preaching Sermons*, 81ff; Vines, *Practical Guide*, 60ff.

4. Taylor, *Next America*, vii.

more low-wage and high-wage jobs, but fewer in between. Our middle class is shrinking. . . . The fastest-growing household type in America contains just one person. Not far behind are multigenerational households, in which two or more adult generations live under the same roof, often because that's the only way to make ends meet.[5]

Indeed, America is changing. The winter winds are blowing across our country and right into our churches. Ignorance about our audience will only waste our opportunity with the snow.

Perhaps the largest single factor to our audience analysis and subsequent sermon shaping will be generational consideration. Now, overgeneralizations abound in these sociological discussions, but ignoring the widely observed, albeit sometimes flawed, distinctives will only create sermons grounded in one generational sweet spot, that is, the preacher's generation. We can ill afford to build a church in our likeness. Christ, the head of the church, would not approve.[6]

Generations Dictate the Carrot Nose or Coal Eyes

The general shape of the snowman has been agreed upon for a long time—one large snowball on the bottom, a medium size snowball for the torso, and a smaller snowball on top for the head.[7] What often varies in the snowman presentation is how they are dressed up. Will there be a carrot nose, a button nose, or a cherry nose? Will there be coals placed for the eyes or will stones do? Should there be a corncob pipe? What about a top hat and scarf?[8]

Sermons likewise have a great many questions surrounding their shape. It depends in large part to whom you are displaying the sermon.

---

5. Ibid., 4.

6. "And he (Jesus) is the head of the body, the church; he is the beginning and the firstborn from among the dead, so that in everything *he might have the supremacy*" (Col 1:18, NIV, italics mine).

7. This site claims that "Frosty is the ultimate authority on snowmen," and he encourages the three sizes of snowballs. See Avery, "How to Build a Snowman," www.sportinglife360.com/index.php/how-to-build-a-snowman-4-17972/.

8. The popular song "Frosty the Snowman" often dictates the cultural norm here: a corncob pipe, button nose, coal eyes, and an old silk hat. See for yourself: "Frosty the Snowman," www.youtube.com/watch?v=pmuJDmjq-xQ.

Each generation of Christians has an outlook that is affected by the decisions you make in the study.

The "Builder generation" describes those people born before 1946.[9] They grew up in the midst of world wars, vast economic swings, and great change. Many Builders enjoyed Abbott and Costello on the radio, sock hops at the YMCA, baseball in an open field, and the emergence of Ford automobiles on the roads. Builders introduced new vocabulary and slang to our nation. Excellent things were *the bee's knees,* scary things gave you the *heebie-jeebies,* and if your boss, or *the big cheese,* liked your work or style, he'd call you *the cat's meow.* Like their language, the Builders' music varied from the "Chattanooga Choo Choo" (Glen Miller Orchestra, 1941) to "A Bushel and a Peck" (Perry Como and Betty Hudson, 1950) to "That'll Be the Day" (Buddy Holly and the Crickets, 1956).

Builders bring to their sermon engagement a strong work ethic. With the emergence of the Industrial Age and the growth of factories and industry, hard work was required to survive in poor economic times. Builders work hard. There is nothing cheap or temporary about their contributions. They are the ones who coined the phrase, "If the job is worth doing, it's worth doing well."

Builders also engage through the lens of stewardship. The Great Depression and the rationing of World War II taught Builders to save anything that might have value and spend frugally. You never knew when you might need that piece of string, bar of soap, or piece of metal. The stock market crash and bank closures created a caution to save money rather than spend it. Parents tried to save money to leave an estate to their children. So Builders planted gardens and canned food. Things were mended and repaired rather than thrown away. They still use the phrase: "Use it up; wear it out; make it do or do without."

Theirs was not a "me" generation as much as a "we" generation. Builders go out of their way to help neighbors and support each other in times of need. They are loyal in their work and voting, loyal to their family secrets ("We don't air our dirty laundry in public"), and loyal in their church attendance. They value Bible study and often think that if someone knows enough Bible, then they will do the right thing. And they have weathered a lot of change. Win Arn, writing about this generation, says, "We were here before pantyhose, drip-dry clothes, icemakers, dishwashers, clothes

---

9. McIntosh, *One Church,* 27ff.

dryers, freezers and electric blankets."[10] Many Builders were also born before the television, penicillin, Frisbees, hula hoops, frozen foods, Xerox, radar, credit cards, ballpoint pens, air conditioning, electric typewriters, and computers.

If we are going to shape a sermon that captures the Builder generation, then it had better be informational. We must do (and display) the hard work of Bible study. Because biblical knowledge is a high value, we had better steward each word and leave nothing to waste. We must display loyalty and respect for those experienced in life and faith and in so doing show loyalty, respect, and reverence for our God.[11]

Next, the Boomer generation burst on to the scene from 1946 to 1964. When World War II was over, the troops came home, the world was safer, and couples started having babies—lots of babies. There was a huge population spike (a baby boom), and the relative peace of our country fostered prosperity and affluence for this new generation. So, incredible experiences shaped this generation.

Boomers watched hours of television shows like *Leave it to Beaver, I Love Lucy,* and *Bonanza.* Music shaped their senses. With the emergence of rock'n'roll and *American Bandstand,* the sounds that shaped a generation came from Elvis Presley, Jerry Lee Lewis, the Beatles, and the Beach Boys. And Boomers had toys: Hula Hoops and Erector Sets, Play-Doh and Troll Dolls, Mr. Potato Head and Barbie and a Davey Crocket coonskin cap. In 1958 alone, more than $100 million dollars' worth of Davey Crocket hats and guns were sold, and $20 million of hula hoops.[12]

Boomers watched with fascination as our country developed a space program. Over 700 million people, the largest TV audience ever, watched the first men walk on the moon on July 20, 1969. Neil Armstrong's words echo across this generation: "That's one small step for man, one giant leap for mankind." Yet, growing up with the hostility of the Cold War, the brutality of racial clashes, and the national upheaval of Vietnam, Boomers grew suspicious of leaders. The assassinations of John F. Kennedy and Martin Luther King Jr. smashed any Camelot utopian dreams.[13]

10. Arn, *Live Long,* 62.

11. "Rise in the presence of the aged, show respect for the elderly and revere your God" (Lev 19:32).

12. McIntosh, *One Church,* 70–71.

13. So many things shaped the Boomers that space won't allow any more discussion, including such generational hallmarks as Watergate, the OPEC energy crisis, and the Grateful Dead.

Boomers engage with sermons that have a crafted, educational feel. This generation attained the highest education levels of any generation up to their time. Nearly twenty-five percent have a college degree, compared to only nine percent of people in the Builder generation. But though they want education, it better not be boring. Boomers are perhaps the most quality-conscious generation in our churches. Because they grew up in prosperous times, they expect nice things. They are the generation that pushed manufacturers to produce quality cars, quality homes, and quality restaurants. They have pushed the church to have a nice nursery, comfortable seating, good air conditioning, and quality programs. What was considered a luxury by their parents is expected by them.

So, if we are going to shape a sermon that captures the Boomer generation, then we had better bring an excellence to our presentation. Our biblical leadership will be called into question if our exposition is awkward and underdeveloped. Words alone won't excite this generation. Action is important. Visuals are important. We had better craft each message with creative and persuasive flair to demonstrate our competence with the most important subject matter in the world.

Generation X crept into our world from 1965 to 1983.[14] As Chuck Underwood writes:

> These are the latch-key kids who grew up street-smart but isolated, often with divorced or career-focused parents. Entrepreneurial. Independent. Creative. Government and big business mean little to them. They are eager to make marriage work and "be there" for their children. They want to save the neighbourhood [sic] if not the world. They are cynical of major institutions who disappointed them and/or their parents. They don't feel like a generation but they are.[15]

That's why they are called Generation X. Like a math formula, X is the unknown quantity that they are trying to discover. And maybe they still are. As Bono from the group U2 expressed in his 1987 hit song, "I still haven't found what I'm looking for."[16] Because Generation X'ers generally don't like labels, it would be better to explore this group through some experiences that shaped them. For instance, music progressed and took new turns. After the disco era of the late 1970's, music became televised on MTV. Video and

---

14. Ibid., 121ff.

15. Underwood, *Generational Imperative*.

16. U2, "I Still Haven't Found What I'm Looking For."

audio blended together.[17] Rock 'n' roll progressed; Bruce Springsteen and Rick Springfield emerged. Journey became popular (the first time around) and Michael Jackson wore one white glove. X'ers left at home played with GI Joes, Transformers, Smurfs, He-Man, Cabbage Patch Dolls, Care Bears, and Strawberry Shortcake, all the while exploring that deep philosophical question posed by Arnold Jackson: "What ch'you talkin' 'bout, Willis?"

Generation X'ers watched traditional authorities fall. Institutions built by the Builder generation and rebelled against by the Boomers crumbled before Generation X. They watched the space program crumble when the *Challenger* exploded in midair. They watched families crumble: nearly forty percent of Gen. X'ers come from parents of divorce.[18] Between forty and fifty percent lived in a single-parent home. Someone from this generation is three times as likely to come from a broken home as their grandparents. Also, they watched societal authority crumble. The Iran Contra scandal shook government authority, Jimmy Swaggert and Jim Bakker shook religious authority, and the Savings and Loans crises shook business authority.

So, many Gen. X'ers grew up cynical, detached, and pessimistic. They bonded with peers more than parents. They became expressive and experiential. They got tattoos like their grandpa and earrings like their grandma. While other generations heard about world events on the radio or TV reports, Generation X watched it happen live—the Space Shuttle *Challenger* explosion, the Berlin Wall dismantled, the Persian Gulf War, and O. J. Simpson's slow-speed chase.

So, if we are going to shape a sermon that captures Generation X, then we had better draw them into a positive experience. Words from an authority figure that may draw a Builder or a visual presentation from a charismatic, spiritual CEO that may draw a Boomer won't crack this generation's attention. Rather, Generation X needs to *experience* a sermon. Through hands-on props or movie clips, they must be drawn into the story. Preachers of Gen. X-sensitive sermons must model maturity as well as preach it. Keep in mind that whereas the Boomers had TV role models like Ward Cleaver, Ozzie Nelson, and the Waltons, Gen. X grew up with such family examples as *The Simpsons*, *Rosanne*, *Married with Children*, and *Mamma's Family*. Gen. X is not Phil Donahue; they are Jerry Springer. So, we had

17. One unfortunate by-product of this turn was that "video killed the radio star" (the Buggles, "Video Killed the Radio Star").

18. McIntosh, *One Church*, 132.

better shape messages that draw them in and introduce them tangibly to the most trustworthy leader in the heavens and the earth.

The Millennial generation began their move into our world starting around 1983.[19] They are a unique group that has experienced a surging cultural landscape marked by change. Every year, Beloit College releases the Beloit College Mindset List, providing a look at the cultural touchstones that shape the lives of students entering college. In their Mindset List for the Class of 2015, they noted these common characteristics:

> There has always been an Internet ramp onto the information highway. Ferris Bueller could be their dad. The phrase "Don't touch that dial!" leads them to ask "what dial?" Refer to LBJ, and they will assume you're talking about LeBron James. They won't go near a retailer that lacks a website. They've often broken up with their significant others via texting, Facebook, or MySpace. They have always cooked popcorn in a microwave.[20]

This is a fascinating generation. Younger millennials have never dialed a rotary phone, played an 8-track, or got up to turn the channel on the TV.

This is a generation marked by a great entrepreneurial spirit and technological playfulness. They have tweeted their way into a new way of viewing the world. Their relational prowess has deep roots as evidenced by a change in children's TV programming that happened when they were kids in 1992. Children's TV went from the urban, rote learning style of Sesame Street to the pastoral, lyrical learning style of one big, purple dinosaur named Barney. How could this generation resist the temptation of becoming hipsters when the song they grew up singing was: "I love you, you love me, we're a happy family, with a great big hug and a kiss from me to you, won't you say you love me too?"[21]

If we are going to shape a sermon that captures Millennials, then we had better get to the point quickly. This generation that can express their feelings in 140 characters or less has little patience for the long oratory and rational argumentation of America's Puritanical past. Sermons must also be authentic and heartfelt. The veneer of happy, posterized religion has been exposed by this generation and they find it lacking. If they can't feel your passion and heart for Jesus, if they can't sense your true feelings on

---

19. Rainer and Rainer, *Millennials*, 2.

20. "The Mindset List for the Class of 2015," www.beloit.edu/mindset/previouslists/2015/.

21. Watch it in all its glory: "I Love You," www.youtube.com/watch?v=FFlkQorzsyE.

the gospel, if they feel that you're holding back unpopular truth to avoid critical backlash, then they will tune you out. This is the generation making Lorde an instant musical success with lyrics confessing: "I'm not proud of my address, in a torn-up town, no postcode envy"[22] or "We live in cities you'll never see on screen, not very pretty, but we sure know how to run things."[23] For this 16-year-old singer, life and success are not about flash (like the Boomer's Beatles and Elvis) or shock (like Generation X's Madonna), but humble authenticity and reality. No wonder many Millennials find the most impactful sermons are those where the guard is dropped (and even the manuscript, gulp!) and truth is spoken honestly from the heart.

Shaping Tools for Sensitive Snowmen

So where does this leave the preacher? There are as many audiences as there are snowflakes, which are piling up in our study demanding to be shaped. How can we take this landscape into account when shaping our sermonic snowmen? Let me offer some shaping tools for those interested in communicating across generations.

The first necessary tool is *intention.* It is imperative that preachers and teachers of God's word make generational distinctions an intentional filter in sermon preparation and delivery. Just as we may anticipate an imagined audience of men and women of different ethnicities, faith backgrounds, and even biblical literacies in our sermon preparation (a practice Dr. Sackett introduced to me), so too we must imagine people of different generations. Then, we must intentionally and routinely offer what is needed to engage each generation in the instruction of God's Word. At times, we must offer unequivocal, biblical information that is precious to the Builder group. Remember that many of the most faithful followers of Jesus in your church belong to a newspaper generation. They enjoy the facts, explained clearly by an authority figure. So, display a map on the screen, tell them the meanings of Hebrew and Greek words, share definitions, and challenge them to memorize Scripture.

Make it your intention to craft an excellent sermon presentation, so cherished by many of our Boomer congregants. Practice your delivery, memorize, and personalize Scripture passages, offer first-person sermon

22. Lorde, "Royals."
23. Lorde, "Team."

presentations[24] on occasion and align sermon themes and worship sets to tell one compelling story. No one despises excellence, but its intentional inclusion may just be the tipping point for someone among the Boomer generation to cross the line of faith.

Intentionally seek to be an inspirational voice for an often apathetic Generation X. With so many reasons to be wary of authority figures in the pulpit, help this generation in your church by garnering honest dialogue from time to time. Share your struggles with the meanings of passages and their application to your life. Don't overwhelm with facts, which this generation can find on Google anyway. Rather, let them see how biblical truth flows into and out of so many areas of life—science, sociology, medicine, business. Locate and express the "context of reality" in the biblical text, which Zack Eswine describes as "the mutual life environment that contemporary believers and unbelievers share in common with those to or about whom the biblical text was written that teaches us about the nature of reality."[25] In other words, utilize current life realities as a bridge into the biblical text. Sometimes, just such an illustration or metaphor from everyday life is a deeply compelling vehicle to thrust a Gen. X'er into a deeper walk of faith.

For a fractured Millennial generation, be intentional about offering short, packed statements of truth. Ask yourself (especially about your homiletical proposition): "Could I tweet this?" Also, don't merely offer tools and models to speak to this generation. Realize that true relationship is always relevant. So whether one uses technology or story or drama or dialogues, remember that it is "our greater love more than our greater technology or techniques that will glorify God and transform a generation."[26] So make intention your first tool. Shape sermons with the generations in mind. Think a newspaper (informational) for Builders, a magazine (presentational) for Boomers, a blog (inspirational) for Generation X, and a tweet (confessional) for Millennials.

A second necessary tool for sermon shaping is *incarnation.* There is no better catalyst for generational sensitivity in sermon preparation than honest conversation and good, old fashioned listening. So, have coffee with people from each generation. Hear their struggles and joys, their desires

24. Robinson and Robinson, *It's All In How You Tell It.* This is the best work I've found on this seldom-used sermon method.

25. Eswine, *Preaching*, 28.

26. Ibid., 84.

and wisdom. Cultivate your ability to speak a common language with each generation. Read magazines targeted at different age groups. Genuinely seek to put yourself in their shoes as a kind of incarnational reflection exercise. Be a missionary at heart, incarnating yourself in each generational culture in order to learn their language, values, dreams, and needs. Then, love them.[27] Such a humble stance models our Master[28] and is a staple of pastoral ministry anyway.

A third tool for sermon shaping is *intuition.* Not only does it take listening ears to hear and live effectively in each generational context, but it also takes a discerning ear to evaluate feedback of your sermons. Some of the greatest evidences of sermon engagement come at the back door of the sanctuary. Dr. Sackett himself opened my eyes to this careful intuiting after sermon delivery. He said that most people will comment, "Good sermon," as they're walking out the door, more as a way to avoid an awkward moment with the preacher. But if someone references your sermon and tells you a story, then you've engaged them.[29]

That has been a great barometer for me. Another one is to listen for some key words that may show a generational shortfall in your preaching. If you hear something like, "the sermon was fluff(y) today" then maybe you're not including enough depth of content and information for the Builders. If you hear "the sermon was a little sloppy" then perhaps the presentational quality didn't meet the excellence standards of our Boomers. If you hear "that sermon was boring" then you've failed to inspire the Generation X'er. If you hear, "the sermon felt fake" then you've not reached the authentic depths that reverberate with the Millennial crowd. Keep your ears open to the feedback offered both formally and informally. It may educate you to a generational need that you can improve upon.

27. Haydn Shaw summarizes how Colin Powell described leading an army: "Love your soldiers. Wake up in the morning and love your soldiers. Go to bed at night thinking about your soldiers." Shaw goes on to say, "Leaders love their people. We can only lead people if we quit trying to change them, and we can't quit trying to change them until we appreciate them, and we can't appreciate them until we understand them. Leadership starts with understanding" (Shaw, *Sticking Points*, 24.) I think ministry and preaching do as well.

28. "Your attitude should be the same as that of Christ Jesus: Who, being in very nature God, did not consider equality with God something to be grasped, but made himself nothing, taking the very nature of a servant, being made in human likeness. And being found in appearance as a man, he humbled himself and became obedient to death—even death on a cross!" (Phil 2:5–8).

29. From one of the class lectures of Dr. Sackett—Homiletics, I believe.

One final tool for generational sermon shaping is immersion. In an interesting article penned about the worship tug-of-war, Dan Wilt distinguishes between a "worship accompaniment" and a "worship immersion" culture in churches. In the area of music, that means that some prefer the music to accompany (read: take a back seat) and support the singing and worship experience, whereas others prefer to be immersed in (read: be surrounded by) the music in worship. This distinction may also help in the sermon portion of a worship experience. He says, "Worship Immersion Culture is not *primarily* drawn to sing *about God*, nor even do they always feel a need to sing *to God*. Rather, they are a generation that wants to sing *with God*. They want to participate in God's life, and be propelled by worship encounters into a world that is begging them to live out their worship incarnationally—manifesting Christ's presence in all aspects of life."[30] For preachers of the word, it may be helpful to consider preaching immersively. We should struggle with the implications of not just preaching about God but preaching with God. What would it mean, for instance, to press people to action after the sermon—to live out this message *with* God instead of merely learning *about* God?[31] Such a mind-set may draw a younger generation to life with God in ways as yet unimagined in your preaching style.

Conclusion

Let me conclude with the twin encouragements of a proverb and a prayer. Just as snowman building has two facets—preparation and presentation—so too we as preachers and teachers of his word need two encouragements. One is an encouraging reality for the preparation of the multigenerational sermon. Proverbs 14:29 says "Whoever is patient has great understanding, but one who is quick-tempered displays folly."

As you continue this journey of preaching, exercise a deep and God-honoring patience. Sometimes generational engagement will be a stellar win and sometimes it will fall flat. Snowmen, like sermons, come and go, season after season. Sometimes building them every week becomes tedious. Preachers can grow weary, questioning whether all of this fuss is worth it.

---

30. Wilt, "Is It Too Loud?," www.danwilt.com/ is-it-too-loud-worship-accompaniment-vs-worship-immersion-culture.

31. See McNeal, *Missional Renaissance*, 102–103, about "debriefing" following a sermon presentation, and Hanson, *Baby Boomers and Beyond*, 164, about providing concrete opportunities for people to practice a preaching challenge.

But trust in God's patient work among all the generations of your church and "be prepared to preach in season and out of season."[32]

The other encouragement is a Pauline prayer: "Now to him who is able to do immeasurably more than all we ask or imagine, according to his power that is at work within us, to him be glory in the church and in Christ Jesus *throughout all generations*, for ever and ever! Amen."[33] God can send and shape, craft and awaken more in people than we can imagine, even across generational lines. His desire is for the church to bring him glory in Christ through all generations. Our work is to shape that word for our context, across each generation, one snowball at a time.

A new generation has pressed this question to us: "Do you wanna build a snowman?"[34] I hope you do. I hope you work and play, craft and shape God's words with all the skill and passion you can muster. Because in the end, every snowman sermon you preach matters. Those snowy sentinels will stand large in your congregation because God promises, "As the rain and the snow come down from heaven, and do not return to it without watering the earth and making it bud and flourish, so that it yields seed for the sower and bread for the eater, so is my word that goes out from my mouth: It will not return to me empty, but will accomplish what I desire and achieve the purpose for which I sent it."[35] Amen!

32. 2 Tim 4:2

33. Eph 3:20–21 (italics mine).

34. Bell, *Do You Want to Build a Snowman?*

35. Isa 55:10–11

12

Multicultural Preaching and Teaching in Eastern Europe

Tony Twist, Fred Hansen

Introduction

TCM International Institute, where Dr. Chuck Sackett has served as an Adjunct Professor of Homiletics and Hermeneutics for two decades, is a graduate level seminary focused on ministry training and discipleship for Russian, European, and Central Asian leaders. Based at Haus Edelweiss, near Vienna, Austria, the Institute has students from thirty-eight countries, speaking twenty-five languages, and classes are taught by professors from ten different countries. Generally speaking, professors teach in English through a translator for a certain language group, although it is not uncommon to have multiple translators for a course. However, even students speaking a common language, such as Russian, come from multiple cultures, such as Russia, Ukraine, Belarus, and many former Soviet bloc countries. Thus, while they may speak the same language, they are not monocultural.

This unique situation presents communicators, whether preachers, teachers, or other volunteers in ministry, with significant opportunities as well as obstacles. The following essay, in honor of Dr. Sackett, seeks to offer brief insights into preparing for effective communication in a multicultural context, as well as highlight some pitfalls.

As the title suggests, this chapter focuses on multicultural preaching and teaching in the Eastern European context. The use of the term multicultural is a conscious effort to distinguish it from other terms, such as cross-cultural and intercultural.[1] While many authors, professors, and practitioners in missiology and sociology use all three terms interchangeably, this is not universal. Nor are definitions of these terms universally accepted and therefore it is desirable to know how the authors will use the terms.[2]

This chapter uses the term multicultural as an environment in which multiple cultures—that is, more than two—interact in a limited fashion. In these environments, understanding other cultures is helpful in communication and personal interactions, but, given its limited scope, does not require the integration of cultures.[3] In other words, a unified culture is not necessarily desired or possible. Such situations do not just occur in places like large, multinational cities. They may occur when several cultures meet for a conference, a class, or a business deal, and have specific, limited goals. At the end of the day or the conference, the various represented groups or individuals retreat back to their own cultures. While one hopes that a multicultural environment fosters respect and understanding for other cultures, the nature of the interaction in such an environment is so limited, intentionally or unintentionally, that integration is not a requisite for individuals or groups to lead successful lives or achieve desired goals.

This is different from intercultural contexts in that those occur when more than two cultures interact in significant, complex, and holistic ways, and seek to integrate as fully as possible with one another. In an intercultural environment, the interactions are total and substantial, such as when several cultures attempt to live in close proximity to one another in a neighborhood or city and adopt and adapt one another's cultural values and norms. In this setting, a person experiences sustained and multiplex

1. The concepts and definitions of the words "multicultural" and "multiculturalism" are hotly debated, so Clayton, *International Encylopedia of Human Geography*, s.v. "Multiculturalism." While recognizing the reality of cultural pluralism in many parts of the world, the terms in this chapter do not suppose the validity or desirability of the ideology of cultural pluralism.

2. The definitions here have some inspiration in those of the United Church of Canada at "Defining Multicultural, Cross-Cultural, and Intercultural," http://www.united-church.ca/files/intercultural/multicultural-crosscultural-intercultural.pdf .

3. Taylor indicates a belief, particularly in Europe, that multiculturalism recognizes differences of cultures living together, but does not encourage integration of these cultures, which one should understand as interculturalism, see Taylor, "Interculturalism or multiculturalism?," 413–423.

relationships with other cultures, which often includes learning a language other than one's first language and affects nearly every facet of one's life. Failure to understand and adapt to the diversity of cultures in this context significantly hinders one's ability to live a fulfilling life.

Lastly, this essay differentiates multicultural from cross-cultural, in that a cross-cultural interaction is when two different cultures contact one another in either a short-term or long-term exchange, and with either a simple or complex acquaintance. Generally, a cross-cultural experience has one dominate culture into which a foreign or less represented culture arrives.

Although TCM International Institute, as a Christian organization, requires its students, staff, professors, and volunteers to love and respect one another and to honor each culture, the limited interaction that exists during classes falls often, though not exclusively, into a multicultural circumstance and therefore this chapter focuses on preaching and teaching in these environments. While love and respect for other cultures successfully aids in short-term interactions, one does not as a matter of necessity have to make the kind of life adjustments necessary for an intercultural exchange.

Preparing for Effective Multicultural Preaching and Teaching[4]

One of the most significant ways in which an individual can prepare for a multicultural communication experience or improve their multicultural communication skills is by developing their cultural intelligence, or CQ.[5] Soon Ang and Linn Van Dyne, pioneers in the theory of cultural intelligence, define CQ as "an individual's capability to function and manage effectively in culturally diverse settings."[6] Ang and Van Dyne further state that CQ is a multidimensional construct consisting of four categories: 1) Metacognitive CQ, "an individual's level of conscious cultural awareness during cross-cultural interactions," 2) Cognitive CQ, which "reflects

---

4. Much of the information shared here is not exclusive to a multicultural context. However, those engaging in intercultural ministry will encounter substantially more complex issues than those presented here.

5. For more on multiple intelligence theory, see Gardner, *Intelligence Reframed*.

6. See Ang and Van Dyne, "Conceptualization," 3. They also note this is consistent with the definition of general intelligence in Schmidt and Hunter, "Select on Intelligence," 3–14, as "the ability to grasp and reason correctly with abstractions (concepts) and solve problems" (Ibid., 3).

knowledge of norms, practices, and conventions in different cultures that has been acquired from educational and personal experiences," 3) Motivational CQ, which "reflects the capability to direct attention and energy toward learning about and functioning in situations characterized by cultural differences," and 4) Behavioral CQ, which "reflects the capability to exhibit appropriate verbal and non-verbal actions when interacting with people from different cultures."[7]

To be fair, Ang and Van Dyne propose that not everyone will have the same level of CQ, just as not everyone possesses the same IQ.[8] One's CQ is often related to "issues of abilities or capabilities, personality, and interests."[9] However, while some individuals will possess a greater CQ than others, perhaps as much by the gifting of the Holy Spirit as personality or interests, anyone preparing for multicultural communication in a Christian context, regardless of their abilities, personality, or interests, should work to address the four dimensions of CQ given above.

While Ang and Van Dyne, along with Koh, go on to propose a complex scientific scale for assessing and developing CQ,[10] called the Cultural Intelligence Scale (CQS), it appears possible to make some general application from their approach as it relates to preaching and teaching in a multicultural context.

Rearranging the four quadrants of CQ, the Motivational CQ aspect figures to be the logical and seminal quadrant within which to begin increasing one's CQ. Since this requires that one "direct[s] attention and energy toward cultural differences,"[11] an individual must assess whether or not they have the desire or ability to expend this energy. If one does not enjoy or desire the process and content of learning more about cultural differences, as below in the Cognitive CQ category, he or she should seriously reconsider whether multicultural interactions are wise.

Furthermore, since the CQS also examines attitudes such as joy and confidence in cultural interactions, it is appropriate within the realm of

7. Ibid., 5–6.

8. Ibid., 7–10.

9. Ibid., 7–8.

10. Although missiologists and missionaries alike are probably already aware of many of the dimensions in the CQ scale of Ang, Van Dyne, and Koh, theirs, along with the many other theoretical scales they draw upon, are helpful in their systematic and holistic approach to assessment, see Van Dyne, Ang, and Koh, "Development and Validation," 16–38.

11. Ibid., 17.

spiritual giftedness to ask whether or not preaching and teaching in a multicultural context brings a person joy or fulfillment. While preachers and teachers may feel a sense of obligation to communicate in such contexts regardless of these feelings, joy and fulfillment are critical to the success of any Christian communicator in a foreign context, particularly if it is sustained to the degree of becoming a long-term intercultural interaction.

If one possesses a certain sense of motivation, then Cognitive CQ is an easier segment of preparation. Here one recommends that any preacher or teacher in a multicultural context learn as much about the cultural differences that exist between themselves and the audience as possible. Where the number of cultures in a particular interaction increases, the preparation is more complex.

Rogers and Steinfatt, in writing of intercultural communication, argue that "Context is a key element in both communication and culture. In order to understand any culture, we must begin with the context that shaped the tools developed to survive in a particular environment, and the definitions of the symbols of verbal and non-verbal communication."[12] In writing about context, they address what they call the "collective cultural consciousness," or those historical events which fundamentally shape the way a culture defines itself.[13] They give as an example the Holocaust and its subsequent effects on the "collective cultural consciousness of Judaism."[14]

Those preaching and teaching in Eastern Europe would do well to familiarize themselves with at least some of the major historical events of its many countries. Since most of these nations were either former Soviet bloc countries, or Soviet sympathizers, much of their modern population is still affected in one way or another by Communist policies. Certainly Gorbachev's politics of *glasnost* and *perestroika* and the subsequent dissolution of the Soviet Union are important aspects of each country's recent history, particularly Russia, Ukraine, Belarus, and so forth.[15]

---

12. Rogers and Steinfatt, *Intercultural Communication*, 1.

13. Ibid., 3. Rogers and Steinfatt write of the embedded memory of these moments within a culture and one could draw upon theories of social memory to understand how, why, and to what end various generations pass these memories on to posterity.

14. Ibid., although one may disagree with the way in which they use the term Judaism.

15. A significant danger arises in these contexts to Americans who are more interested in capitalism and the West than Christianity and heavenly citizenship. Arrogant boasts declaring the supremacy of capitalism and the US have no place in Christian interactions, particularly with other Christians in these parts of the world.

As an example of the events of the fall of Communism, on his first visit to Bucharest, one of the authors discovered that many Romanian Christians often speak of former Communist leader Nicolae Ceausescu and his execution, along with his wife Elena, on December 25, 1989. While this event doesn't dominate daily conversation, they repeatedly mentioned the final days of Ceausescu's rule when asked about the defining moments or issues of their current state of affairs.[16]

Another important matter that arose when asking Romanians about their collective consciousness was the territory of Transylvania and its Hungarian population. Transylvania is a long-disputed area between Romania and Hungary, populated by both Hungarians and Romanians. Many individuals living in that part of Romania will introduce themselves as Hungarians by ethnicity and Romanians by nationality and are quite fluent in both languages. Failure to recognize this situation can lead to some difficult and awkward conversational situations.

In both Romanian examples, Ceausescu and Transylvania appear as important to the current collective consciousness of Romania as September 11, 2001 is to the citizens of the United States. Moreover, these deeply held memories, as well as more recent current events, may serve as helpful illustrations in sermons or lessons if one uses them properly. Particularly in the case of current events, demonstrating awareness of what is happening in the lives and countries of the audience is an excellent way to show interest, compassion, and grace. Asking individuals native to a particular culture about the impact of historical and current events gives a preacher or teacher more credibility, as merely reading about these events still subjects the communicator to interpreting these events only through his or her own cultural lens. This simple research and listening goes a long way to improving one's Cognitive CQ and provides a basic framework in which to place additional information gleaned through interaction.

At a very practical level, once a preacher or teacher gleans additional information about a culture through various forms of media as well as

16. This situation provided a helpful insight. When preaching or teaching, ask the audience, preferably before (but even sometimes during) a sermon or lesson, to define these moments. Their personal experiences and understanding of events is often vastly different from that which one reads in historical accounts or views in documentaries. On this particular visit in the summer of 2013, while touring Bucharest after teaching courses in the New Testament, students recurrently showed their professor the balcony from which Ceausescu spoke on December 21, 1989, which overlooks what they call in English "Revolution Square."

interpersonal contact, this knowledge provides a helpful starting place for illustrations and analogies within sermons and lessons. Far too many Western preachers and teachers find that their illustrations and analogies of biblical texts are so culturally rooted as to prove useless, or worse, dangerous. This propensity for extreme cultural relevance, rooted only in the culture of the speaker, through the use of popular movies, music, and television programs in one's own culture, is quite limiting when it comes to multicultural communication. The things that make a preacher popularly relevant in one culture may make him anathema in another.[17] Choosing illustrations and analogies that are rooted in shared humanity (everyone experiences pain, suffering, loss, and joy, for instance), coupled with additional study about the events and values of each culture aids in limiting any cultural faux pas which may occur.[18] For example, one of the authors of this chapter observed Chuck Sackett preach a sermon in a multicultural context using an extensive wedding illustration in which the story from the perspective of the bride of visibly affected most participants.

While assessing Motivational CQ and improving Cognitive CQ may be first steps in multicultural interactions, Metacognitive CQ and Behavioral CQ are likely to be more difficult quadrants to address, as these require higher levels of self-awareness.

Metacognitive CQ requires that one is consciously aware that different cultural dynamics are at work in any interaction with members of other cultures. This self-awareness is related to Cognitive CQ, in that the awareness derives from knowledge. Metacognitive awareness then drives Behavioral CQ. As one is aware of the cultural dynamics, then one can conscientiously adjust his or her behavior appropriately in each situation. This behavioral adjustment may be quite fluid even in a short period of time

17. For instance, many Eastern European Christians may not watch programs or movies from the West. Many of those who have attempted to do so may find them decadent and immoral. Using illustrations rooted in these experiences may cause the audience to think the preacher or teacher is less than moral. Each situation is different, but on the whole, it is safer to limit these types of references.

18. Rockstuhl and NG effectively argue that improving one's CQ helps "to overcome negative reactions and misunderstandings that arise from social categorization processes" (Rockstuhl and NG, "Effects of Cultural Intelligence," 209). In other words, the preacher or teacher is viewed less as an outsider and more as one who cares about the audience. At a far more complex level, examining one's theology as it is culturally rooted as well as the culturally rooted theology of the audience is an important aspect of preaching and teaching. A short, yet helpful example of culturally rooted Christology is in Montgomery-Fate, *Mission*, 72–80.

as one must, at times, work to adjust behavior in the moment, in order to better communicate and relate.

An example of how this Metacognitive CQ and Behavioral CQ is significant in preaching and teaching is with respect to nonverbal communication, such as posture, dress, and gestures.[19] For instance, while it may be common in a Western context for a preacher or teacher to place his or her hands in the pockets of their pants while communicating, such an act may be regarded as insulting and careless in some Eastern European contexts.[20]

Since Rogers and Steinfatt are correct in asserting that it is impossible to avoid nonverbal communication, it is important for multicultural communicators to learn as much as possible about nonverbal communication in particular cultures, thus raising their Cognitive CQ.[21] They must also be aware of these nonverbal cues in communicating, demonstrating a high Metacognitive CQ, and appropriately act on this information when preaching, thereby indicating a high Behavioral CQ. One very interesting illustration of the need for this comes from a mealtime at Haus Edelweiss when an American table hostess continually gave the Bulgarian students exactly the food they did not want. Only later did she discover that nodding the head up and down in Bulgaria means "no" and side-to-side nodding of the head means "yes!"

---

19. Rogers and Steinfatt, quoting studies by Mehrabian and Ferris, argue that nonverbal communication accounts for as much as 93 percent of interpreted meaning in everyday communications, though other studies suggest about 66 percent. They also posit that the more technical the level of communication is, the less important nonverbal communication is (Rogers and Steinfatt, *Intercultural Communication*, 162). Martin and Nakayama include facial expressions, personal space, eye contact, use of time, and conversational silence as other forms of nonverbal communication with which communicators must be aware in *Experiencing Intercultural Communication*, 170.

20. One difficult situation that one of the authors faced in Eastern Europe in 2009 relates to the wearing of a wedding band on the left hand in the USA. In this particular European context, divorced individuals wear their old wedding rings on the left hand ring finger. One Christian student was concerned that a divorced professor was teaching a course in the New Testament. His interpretation of a nonverbal situation was entirely unlike that of a Westerner and a short-lived relational rift ensued.

21. Rogers and Steinfatt, *Intercultural Communication*, 164. An area that many in the US may find particularly emotional is the role of body piercings and tattoos. While they are becoming popular among younger generations in the US and even many preachers have piercings and tattoos, these communicate nonverbally and are interpreted very differently in other cultures. As much as they may help in one context, they may be a hindrance in another (Martin and Nakayama, *Experiencing Intercultural Communication*, 173).

Thus, the more information, awareness, and appropriate behavioral adjustment a communicator demonstrates, the higher the level of CQ, and therefore the increased chances of communicative success when preaching and teaching in a multicultural context. It has been the observation of both authors of this chapter that Chuck Sackett has continually demonstrated by example a very high level of CQ throughout his many years of teaching and preaching throughout Eastern Europe.

13

Leading a Congregation through Preaching

Don Green

A Tribute

SOME PREACHERS ARE ABLE to preach well. A few of these preachers are capable of teaching others to preach well. Then there are the rare preachers and teachers of preachers who are also able to lead well. Chuck Sackett is one of those who preaches, teaches, and leads well; and this writer has observed him doing it for more than thirty years. The premise of this chapter is that effective preaching involves not only *feeding* the sheep but also *leading* the flock. This chapter will explore how one leads a congregation through preaching and will address such vital areas as casting vision, communicating values, and energizing followers from the pulpit. It will focus on John Kotter's description of the leadership task of establishing direction, aligning people, and motivating and inspiring. Finally, Dr. Sackett's preaching plan for 2013 will be examined to illustrate how planned preaching is an effective and essential means of leading a congregation.

Biblical leadership is defined as "taking the initiative to know God deeply, to reflect His holy character abundantly and through loving relationships to draw people together to further His purposes in the world."[1] Chuck Sackett is, by that definition, a Biblical leader. Those who know him well know that he consistently seeks to know God deeply, through his per-

1. Saffold, Coursepack for DMin. Course 880A, *Theology of Leadership*, 38.

sonal study of Scripture and his personal relationship with Jesus Christ. Those who have encountered him in a classroom or in a congregational setting have seen how he reflects God's holy character abundantly. Fellow leaders and staff members who serve with him in ministry would attest that as a leader, he intentionally invests himself in relational leadership in order to draw people together. And anyone who knows Chuck's heart for the kingdom knows that his desire is not to further his purposes, but God's purposes in the world.

In addition to being a Biblical leader, he also understands the relationship of leading and preaching. In his popular seminary course, *Leading from the Pulpit*, Dr. Sackett "explores how Biblical proclamation leads a congregation in accomplishing the church's stated mission."[2] His stated rationale for this course is, "The pulpit is the most dominant voice in the congregation. What is said there dictates the direction and action of the congregation. Intentional preaching moves the church to be and do what the leadership desires it to be and do."[3] Before examining how Dr. Sackett accomplishes this leadership task in his own preaching, it would serve the purposes of this chapter to see the relationship of preaching and leading from a Biblical perspective and to more clearly define the task of leading.

The Text

John. V. Tornfelt laments "how little has been written about leadership's relationship to preaching. . . . Scan the literature base and you find a dearth of material. While some thought has been given to their relationship, it is vague and limited. And though the homileticians may be silent, the Scriptures are not."[4] Leading and preaching are joined together in Scripture not only by example in the lives of such preacher/leaders as Jeremiah, Peter, Paul, Timothy, and Titus, but also in Paul's description of elders: "The elders who direct the affairs of the church well are worthy of double honor, especially those whose work is preaching and teaching" (1 Tim 5:17, NIV). The word translated "direct the affairs of the church" (*proistēmi*) "occurs only in Paul, and six out of his eight uses of the verb refer to officers and their activity in the church (Rom 12:8; 1 Thess 5:12; 1 Tim 3:5; 5:17) or in their family (1 Tim 3:4, 12), the latter serving as proof of their ability

2. Sackett, Syllabus for Course PR660 *Leading from the Pulpit*.

3. Ibid.

4. Tornfelt, "Preaching and Leading," 2.

to lead the church (1 Tim 3:4–5)."[5] Literally translated "to stand before," this word "emphasizes the leadership role of one who has been placed at the head of the family or church and who is therefore responsible to 'rule, direct and lead'. . . and 'be concerned about' or 'care for' (as in Tit 3:8, 14)."[6] The elders (*presbyteroi*), to be so honored, labor in word and teaching (*en logō kai didaskalia*). "Word" is often understood as the act of "speaking." Knight rightly observes, "most modern English translations have correctly rendered it here as 'preaching' in the sense of exhortation and application."[7] While some authors make a distinction between elders who oversee (ruling elders) and elders who preach and teach (teaching elders), among the qualities expected of any elder is that he be "able to teach." (1 Tim 3:2). It seems more plausible that some elders whose work requires full-time devotion to the preaching/teaching task are the ones who are worthy of remuneration. Kelly notes,

> This text suggests that a distinction is beginning to emerge between the main body of elders who wield this general oversight and the narrower group amongst them who have more specific tasks to perform. This . . . is probably implied in the expression who exercise leadership well. By this must be meant, not simply those who have proved good elders (the quality of their service cannot have been the basis of a difference in remuneration), but those who have taken an active and efficient, possibly full-time share in administration. The most obvious examples of these must have been those occupied in preaching and teaching.[8]

Eugene Peterson paraphrases this charge to Timothy as, "Give a bonus to leaders who do a good job, especially the ones who work hard at preaching and teaching."[9]

Although Scripture does not provide an exact parallel to the contemporary preaching minister of a local congregation, the leadership task is noted in such texts as Heb 13:7, "Remember your leaders, who spoke the word of God to you. Consider the outcome of their way of life and imitate their faith," and Heb 13:17, "Obey your leaders and submit to their authority. They keep watch over you as men who must give an account. Obey

5. Knight, *Pastoral Epistles*, 232.

6. Ibid., 161.

7. Ibid., 233.

8. Kelly, *Pastoral Epistles*, 124.

9. Peterson, *Message*, 1643.

them so that their work will be a joy, not a burden, for that would be of no advantage to you." The leaders depicted here are accountable overseers (a word used interchangeably with elders and shepherds or pastors in such places as Acts 20:17, 28 and I Pet 5:1–2) who are responsible for speaking (preaching and teaching) the Word of God.

Michael Quicke includes this idea of leading in his definition of preaching: "Christian preaching, at its best, is a biblical speaking/listening/seeing/hearing/doing event that God empowers to lead and form Christ-shaped people and communities."[10] One could argue that leading well from a spiritual perspective and in a Christian context is not only connected with preaching and teaching but is dependent upon the Word. As Quicke notes, "Leadership left to its own devices can lose spiritual footing in several ways. Separation from preaching increases the dangers of leadership degenerating into humanistic advice, becoming devoid of the Holy Spirit, empty of spiritual understanding, and predisposed to puffed up pride."[11] As the task of leadership is framed from a secular perspective in the following section, it is not intended that church leaders should seek to do so apart from the centrality of the Word.

The Task

Although several different words are used in the New Testament to define the function of leading,[12] specific leadership tasks are not clearly defined. This is where the church can glean insight from contemporary voices.[13] Beyond the work of serving, stewarding, shepherding, overseeing, preaching, teaching, and modeling Christlike maturity, how do elders and preaching ministers lead their congregations?

In his seminal work, John P. Kotter makes a clear distinction between managing and leading. What he observed about most US corporations can also be said of many churches in America: "[they] are overmanaged and underled."[14] Kotter's distinction between management and leadership is seen in the following table:[15]

10. Quicke, *360-Degree Leadership*, 52.

11. Ibid., 62.

12. See Bennett, *Metaphors of Ministry.*

13. Quicke, *360-Degree Leadership*, 11.

14. Kotter, *Force for Change*, 3.

15. Ibid., 139.

Management	Leadership
Planning/Budgeting	Establishing Direction
• Details and Timetables	• Vision of the Future
• Allocating Resources	• Strategies for Change
Organizing/Staffing	Aligning People
• Organizational Structure	• Communicating Directions
• Staffing	• Influencing Words & Deeds
• Delegating Responsibility	• Teams "On Board"
• Policies and Procedures	
• Monitoring Systems	
Controlling/Problem Solving	Motivating/Inspiring
• Results vs. Plans	• Energizing People
• Identifying Deviations	• Overcoming Barriers
• Solving Deviations	• Fulfillment
Coping with complexity	*Creating change*
Produces degree of predictability and order/key results	*Produces change, often dramatic, and effective results*

It is this author's opinion that elders and preaching ministers must be about the task of providing leadership for the overall ministry of a church, while empowering other servants (ministry staff, deacons, or other servant leaders) to manage the various ministries of the church. In a *Harvard Business Review* article entitled "What Leaders Really Do," Kotter observes, "What leaders really do is prepare organizations for change and help them cope as they struggle through it."[16] The three specific tasks of leadership are essential elements in preparing for and leading through change. "Since the function of leadership is to produce change, setting the direction of that change is fundamental to leadership."[17] Alignment is essential to avoid conflict of competing agendas, or as Kotter notes, "Unless many individuals line up and move together in the same direction, people will tend to fall all over one another."[18] "Just as direction setting identifies an appropriate path for movement and just as alignment gets people moving down that path,

16. Kotter, "What Leaders Really Do," 3.

17. Ibid., 5.

18. Ibid., 7.

successful motivation ensures that they will have the energy to overcome obstacles."[19] He draws an important connection between vision and values as he notes, "Good leaders motivate people in a variety of ways. First, they always articulate the organization's vision in a manner that stresses the values of the audience they are addressing."[20] These specific tasks of establishing direction, aligning people, and motivating and inspiring are accomplished in part through preaching.

A trio of church consultants, and coauthors of the book *Leading Congregational Change*, Mike Bonem, Jim Herrington, and James Furr, describe the vital role of the pastor (preaching minister) in leading a congregation through change in the foreword of *360-Degree Leadership: Preaching to Transform Congregations*: "the pastor has the specific biblical role of teaching, equipping, and leading the local body of believers. . . . the pastor has far more opportunity than anyone else to influence the spiritual health and the strategic direction of the church. After all, who else is actively involved in the key decisions and also able to exhort the entire body each week?"[21]

Being in the Word and engaging in effective preaching/teaching provide the needed context for navigating change in a changing culture. Discerning what must never change in terms of the church's message and mission and what must change in terms of methodology and strategy is a vital leadership task. Preaching provides the congregational leader a unique venue for casting vision in ways that connect with core values shared by the congregation. Quicke makes an astute observation as he provides an overview of church leadership literature: "Much of the extensive literature on church leadership has little or nothing good to say about preaching having a leadership role."[22] He concludes, "Most writing on Christian leadership omits preaching, and most books on preaching leave out leadership. For many everyday pastors in ordinary churches this displacement of preaching has brought bewilderment and anxiety. The eclipse of preaching/leading has torn out the heart of the Christian ministry"[23] He coins the term "thin-blooded preaching" to describe this "type of preaching that misses

19. Ibid., 9.
20. Ibid.
21. Quicke, *360-Degree Leadership*, 11.
22. Ibid., 28.
23. Ibid., 30.

out on leadership."[24] He characterizes this preaching that is void of leading and which ultimately undoes Christian leadership as:

1. Individualistic

2. Aimed at Head or Heart but Rarely Both Together

3. Spineless Theology

4. Generic Application

5. Avoids Conflict

6. Low Compliance

7. Absence of Process Issues

8. Solo Role

9. Cowardice

10. Missionally Defective[25]

He concludes that the aspiration of effective preacher/leaders "should be to proclaim truth that is corporate as well as individual, specific in intent, and healthily honest about conflict. They should seek high commitment and collaborate with others as well as engage in process issues and show holy boldness. . . . Preaching must rediscover its power to lead people together in a penetrating, life altering way."[26]

In the church context, a leadership team comprised of elders and the preaching minister provides the overall direction and "big picture" perspective for the church. In a healthy leadership team a preaching minister serves and leads alongside elders as an equal among equals. Typically, the preaching minister is the one who primarily casts the collective vision of the elders to the congregation. This role is consistent with Elton Trueblood's description of the role of the pastor as a "player coach"[27] and with Paul's reference to equipping "pastor-teachers" in Eph 4:11 as well as to those elders who are "worthy of double honor" and "whose work is preaching and teaching" in 1 Tim 5:17.

---

24. Ibid., 34.

25. Ibid., 34–38.

26. Ibid., 42

27. Trueblood, *Incendiary Fellowship*, 41.

An Example of Effective Leading through Preaching

What does leading a congregation through preaching look like? Tornfelt poses these questions about the preaching-leading task:

> And so if preaching and leading do belong together, in what ways? How does the pulpit impact a pastor's capacity to lead? What is the relationship between preaching and providing vision, establishing goals and objectives, reaching consensus, gathering financial support, dealing with resistance, and facing conflict?[28]

An examination of sermons preached at the Madison Park Christian Church in Quincy, IL in 2013 will illustrate how Chuck Sackett and his preaching team are leading this congregation through planned preaching. According to the history of Madison Park Christian Church, where Dr. Sackett serves as Preaching Minister, "In 2010, we began to highlight our vision of facilitating life change—something we believe captures the essence of being disciples of Jesus. We adopted a simple threefold strategy to accomplish our mission. We seek to Encounter God in meaningful ways (worship and interaction with God's people), Connect with God's people around God's word (discipling believers), and Serve one another, the community and the world."[29]

The eight series of sermons ranging in length from four to nine messages that were planned and preached during 2013[30] were:

Relentless (January 6–January 27, 2013)

1. Reluctantly Relentless (Jonah 1)
2. Submissively Relentless (Jonah 2)
3. Successfully Relentless (Jonah 3)
4. Compassionately Relentless (Jonah 4)

This series from Jonah clearly cast the vision for what kind of church God wants His church to be and called the congregation to embrace the value of evangelism. The core message of pursuing God's plan and His

28. Tornfelt, "Preaching and Leading," 3.

29. "Our History," http://madisonparkchurch.com/about/history/.

30. "Messages," http://sermons.madisonparkchurch.com/show_all_sermons. php?pass_year=&sunday_only=T.

people captured God's heart with the recurring theme, "I want everyone. I want all of them." As Tornfelt observes,

> First, a realistic vision for the future can be communicated through preaching. Prone to be comfortable and self-protective, people need continual reminders they are a people of mission, who are responsibly to engage the world with the gospel (Matt 28:19–20). Tragically, time has a way of eroding a church's sense of purpose.[31]

These four sermons demonstrated that there is no better way to begin a new year than to remind the congregation of its eternal task and to do it through the captivating story of Jonah.

Resident Aliens (February 3–March 24, 2013)

1. The Relentless Pursuit of Community (1 Pet 1:1–2)

2. Living as Redeemed Aliens in a Changing World (1 Pet 1:3–12)

3. Creating Distinctive Communities of Faith (1 Pet 1:13–21)

4. Love: A Distinctive Quality of Christian Community (1 Pet 1:22–23)

5. A Community Created by a Powerful Word (1 Pet 1:24–25)

6. A Community Created by a Good Word (1 Pet 1:25)

7. A Community Created by a Nourishing Word (1 Pet 2:1–3)

8. A Community Captivated by a Captivating Word (Mark 11)

9. Living in the Power of the Rejected One (1 Pet 2:4–8)

Redefining Church (April 7–May 19, 2013)

1. We are God's People (1 Pet 2:9–10)

2. We are God's People Giving God Honor (1 Pet 2:9)

3. God's People Redeemed by God's Mercy (1 Pet 2:10)

4. God's People on God's Mission (1 Pet 2:11–12)

5. God's People on God's Mission in the Neighborhood (1 Pet 2:13–17)

---

31. Tornfelt, "Preaching and Leading," 3.

6. God's People on God's Mission in the Workplace (1 Pet 2:18–25)

7. God's People on God's Mission in the Home (1 Pet 3:1–7)

Hope from the Margins (May 26–June 30, 2013)

1. The Church Characterized by Hope (1 Pet 3:8–12)

2. The Church Characterized by Doing Good (1 Pet 3:13–17)

3. The Church Characterized by Leaving the Past (1 Pet 3:18–4:6)

4. The Church Characterized by Material Generosity (1 Pet 4:7–11)

5. The Church Characterized by Relational Generosity (1 Pet 4:7–19)

6. A Church Characterized by Godly Leadership (1 Pet 5:1–5)

These twenty-two messages from 1 Peter were preached in three thematic series. The first series focused on what it means to be the people of God. Again, the vision is cast for "a church with an everyday mission that is always on mission." These messages were designed to define what it means to be a community of faith. The third message in the series *Creating Distinctive Communities of Faith* was a collaborative effort that included testimonies from a small group of Christian brothers conveying how life is best lived in community and how important it is for Christians to "do life together," another core value for congregational life. Four of the messages in this series underscored the Word-centered core value of the church, themes that grew out of the text from 1 Peter. Even a casual listener to the messages would catch the centrality of the Word in the life of this congregation as Scripture references are consistently accompanied with page numbers in the reference Bibles provided for the hearers.

The second series of seven messages focused on clarifying the identity of the church as fundamental to fulfilling the mission of the church. The final six messages from 1 Peter addressed some of the cultural and congregational challenges facing the congregation. Not only does preaching lead through casting vision, but "Second, sermons are a means of achieving consensus when decisions must not only be made but supported by the congregation."[32] In these messages the preacher is leading the congregation to support community-based ministries requiring generous stewardship and willing servants.

32. Tornfelt, "Preaching and Leading," 3.

Seeing Jesus (July 7–August 25, 2013)

1. He's It; There's No Other Way

2. You Won't Find It in There (Prince of Peace)

3. No Need to Face Him Alone

4. Yes, It Really Is Him

5. He Did It Again, and He'll Do It Again

6. So Much More than We Ever Imagined

7. A King Who Reigns through Service

8. The Beginning, the End, and Everything in Between
   (Alpha and Omega)

This eight-sermon series using multiple Scripture texts focused on who Jesus is, what he claims, what the Bible says about him, and what he means to the world. This series illustrates another key way that one can lead through preaching: "Third, preaching can force a church to face controversies and thorny issues."[33] Doctrinal preaching serves not only to bring about life change but also to bring disciples to greater obedience and spiritual maturity.

Say What? (September 1–October 6, November 10–November 24)

1. Have Nothing to Do with Non-Christians

2. Money Is the Root of All Evil

3. Did God Really Say We Should Tithe?

4. Only Men Could Lead in the Church

5. Forgive and Forget

6. Whosoever Will

7. God Helps those Who Help Themselves

8. Give It All

9. Does God Really Say that Numbers Aren't Important?

33. Ibid., 4.

The first five of these messages could be categorized as also addressing controversial and thorny issues as the previous series on Jesus. The message *Whosoever Will* is a vison-casting message reminding the congregation of God's passion to pursue lost people. The final three messages were an effective means of accomplishing a final goal of leading through preaching. Tornfelt notes:

> Fourth, preaching can mobilize people for ministry. Whether it is motivating people to serve for the first time or maintaining a commitment, keeping people involved remains a challenge. While men and women may have legitimate reasons to minimize or discontinue involvement, apathy is pervasive. For this reason, preachers have the responsibility to lead by articulating the biblical grounds for servanthood. Efforts to mobilize people should not be harangues or sound like desperate cries for volunteers but be understood as invitations to be co-workers in God's Kingdom.[34]

Without knowing the church calendar, it appeared that the three messages in this series preached during the month of November coincided with challenging the congregation to commit themselves to finish the year strong, affirm a budget, and prepare for the year to come. The message *Does God Really Say that Numbers Aren't Important?* is a textbook example of leading through preaching. As Dr. Sacket drew application from God's concern for numbers in Acts, he challenged the congregation to see beyond a budget to see needs being met, ministries being done, programs being started, ministry staff being added, and decisions for Christ being made. With a stirring reminder of 50,000 unreached people in the area and a call to do all for God's honor, he cast a vision for what could be done in 2014 through the faithfulness of God's people.

Relentless: When God Is in Control
(October 13–November 2, 2013)

1. When God Leads

2. When God Says No

3. When God Is in Control

4. When God Sends

34. Ibid.

This series of four messages was the second series labeled "Relentless" preached in 2013. Like the first series of four messages which focused on Jonah's encounter with God and His mission, through this series taken from such texts as Psa 136; Acts 16:5–10; Isa 6:1–13; and John 20:19–23, the congregation was reminded that God is still on a mission and he sends us to join him in the adventure. The "Relentless" theme built on the vision cast the previous year and the campaign called "Relentless."[35]

Presence: An Advent Series
(December 1–December 29, 2013)

1. Hope

2. Love

3. Joy

4. Peace

5. His Presence Assures Us We Are Saved

The Advent series taken from various texts was a clarion call to finding greater meaning and fulfillment in the message of Christ's coming than contemporary culture offers. Like previous messages which were preached at Madison Park Christian Church in 2013, these messages were crucial to leading the congregation in pursuit of its vision of facilitating life change.

Hopefully, this cursory look at just one year in the planned preaching schedule of Madison Park Christian Church will prompt the reader to listen to the sermons and do a more thorough analysis of how various messages demonstrate leading through preaching. One will find entire messages devoted to establishing direction (casting and communicating vision). Other messages are designed to align God's people by clarifying core values and shared commitments, influencing their words and deeds. Still other messages played a vital role in motivating and inspiring the congregation to accomplish the church's mission through its threefold strategy: "We seek to Encounter God in meaningful ways (worship and interaction with God's people), Connect with God's people around God's word (discipling believers), and Serve one another, the community and the world."[36]

35. "Our History," http://madisonparkchurch.com/about/history/.
36. Ibid.

May what is said of marriage be said of preaching and leading: "What God has joined together let no man put asunder." And may God multiply the impact of Chuck Sackett's preaching, teaching, and leading to raise up a generation of Biblical leaders who can communicate God's Word effectively and in so doing lead their congregations effectively. All for God's glory and for the advancement of his kingdom.

Bibliography

Adams, Sean A. *The Genre of Acts and Collected Biography*. Society for New Testament Studies Monograph Series 156. Cambridge: Cambridge University Press, 2013.

Aberbach, M., and L. Smolar. "Aaron, Jeroboam, and the Golden Calves." *Journal of Biblical Literature* 86 (1967) 129–140.

Akin, Daniel L., Bill Curtis, and Stephen Rummage. *Engaging Exposition*. Nashville: Broadman & Holman, 2011.

Ang, Soon, and Linn Van Dyne. "Conceptualization of Cultural Intelligence: Definition, Distinctiveness, and Nomological Network." In *Handbook of Cultural Intelligence*, edited by Soon Ang and Linn Van Dyne, 3–15 Armonk, NY: M.E. Sharpe, 2008.

Aratus. "Phaenomena." In *Callimachus: Hymns and Epigraphs, Lycophron and Aratus*, translated by A.W. Mair and G.R. Mair, 1:206–299. The Loeb Classical Library 129. Cambridge: Harvard University Press, 1955.

Aristotle. *Aristotle, The Poetics; "Longinus," On the Sublime; Demetrius, On Style*. Translated by W. Hamilton Fyfe. Loeb Classical Library 199. London: William Heinemann, 1928.

Arn, Win. *Live Long and Love It!* Carol Stream, IL: Tyndale House, 1991.

Arthurs, Jeffrey D. *Preaching with Variety*. Grand Rapids: Kregel, 2007.

Augustine. *On Christian Doctrine*. Christian Classics Ethereal Library. http://www.ccel.org/a/augustine/doctrine/.

Avery, Nan C. "How to Build a Snowman." www.sportinglife360.com/index.php/how-to-build-a-snowman-4-17972/.

Bailey, Kenneth. *Poet and Peasant* and *Through Peasant Eyes: A Literary-Cultural Approach to the Parables in Luke*. Combined ed. Grand Rapids: Eerdmans, 1996.

Balswick, Jack O. and Judith K. *The Family*. Grand Rapids: Baker, 1991.

Beach, Nancy. *An Hour On Sunday: Creating Moments of Transformation and Wonder*. Grand Rapids: Zondervan, 2004.

Bell, Kristen. *Do You Want to Build a Snowman?* From *Disney's Frozen Soundtrack*. November 25, 2013.

Bennett, David W. *Metaphors of Ministry: Biblical Images for Leaders and Followers.* Eugene, OR: Wipf & Stock, 2004.

Berlin, Adele. *Poetics and Interpretation of Biblical Narrative.* Winona Lake, IN: Eisenbrauns, 1994.

Bewes, Richard. Interview by Dr. Mark Searby. London, August 1, 2013.

Blomberg, Craig. *Interpreting the Parables.* Downers Grove, IL: IVP, 1990.

Blount, Brian K., and Gary W. Charles. *Preaching Mark in Two Voices.* Louisville: Westminster John Knox, 2002.

Bonhoeffer, Dietrich. "Paper on the Historical and Pneumatological Interpretation of Scripture." In *The Young Bonhoeffer: 1918-1927*, edited by Paul Duane Matheny, Clifford J. Green, and Marshall D. Johnson, translated by Mary C. Nebelsick and Douglas W. Stott, 285–300. Minneapolis: Fortress, 2002.

Borden, Paul, and Steven D. Mathewson. "The Big Idea of Narrative Preaching." In *The Art and Craft of Biblical Preaching*, edited by Haddon Robinson and Craig Brian Larson, 271–280. Grand Rapids: Zondervan, 2005.

Bray, Gerald. "Augustine's Key." *Christian History* 80 (2003) 42–44.

Bruce, F. F. *The Acts of the Apostles: Greek Text with Introduction and Commentary.* Grand Rapids: Eerdmans, 1990.

Brueggemann, Walter. *Great Prayers of the Old Testament.* Louisville: Westminster John Knox, 2008.

The Buggles. *Video Killed the Radio Star.* From the album *The Age of Plastic.* September 7, 1979.

Burridge, Richard A. "The Genre of Acts—Revisited." In *Reading Acts Today: Essays in Honour of Loveday C. A. Alexander*, edited by Steve Walton, Thomas E. Phillips, Lloyd K. Pietersen, and F. Scott Spencer, 3–28. Library of New Testament Studies 427. London: T & T Clark, 2011.

———. *What Are the Gospels?* 2nd ed. Cambridge: Eerdmans, 2004.

Buttrick, David. *Homiletic: Moves and Structures.* Philadelphia: Fortress, 1987.

Butzu, David A., and Bruce E. Shields. *Generations of Praise: The History of Worship.* Joplin, MO: College Press, 2006.

Cairns, Frank. *The Prophet of the Heart: Being the Warrack Lectures on Preaching for 1934.* London: Hodder and Stoughton, 1934.

Carter, Terry G., J. Scott Duvall, and J. Daniel Hays. *Preaching God's Word: A Hands-On Approach to Preparing, Developing, and Delivering the Sermon.* Grand Rapids: Zondervan, 2005.

Cary, Phillip. *Jonah.* Grand Rapids: Brazos, 2008.

Chatman, Seymour. *Story and Discourse: Narrative Structure in Fiction and Film.* London: Cornell University, 1978.

Chapell, Bryan. *Christ-Centered Preaching.* 2nd ed. Grand Rapids: Baker, 1994.

———. *Christ-Centered Preaching: Redeeming the Expository Sermon.* Grand Rapids: Baker, 2005.

———. *Christ Centered Worship: Letting the Gospel Shape Our Practice.* Grand Rapids: Baker, 2009.

Cherry, Constance M. *The Worship Architect: A Blueprint for Designing Culturally Relevant and Biblically Faithful Services.* Grand Rapids: Baker, 2010.

Chisholm, Robert B. "חד," in vol. 1 of *New International Dictionary of Old Testament Theology & Exegesis*, edited by Willem A. VanGemeren, 1048–1050. Grand Rapids: Zondervan, 1997.

Clarke, Andrew D. *A Pauline Theology of Church Leadership.* London: Bloomsbury T & T Clark, 2008.

Clayton, John. *International Encylopedia of Human Geography.* New York: Elsevier, 2009.

Clines, David J. A. *The Theme of the Pentateuch.* 2nd edition. Sheffield: Sheffield Academic Press, 1997.

Cox, Richard H. *Rewiring Your Preaching: How the Brain Processes Sermons.* Downers Grove, IL: IVP, 2012.

Craddock, Fred B. *Preaching.* Nashville: Abingdon, 1985.

Culpepper, R. Alan. *Anatomy of the Fourth Gospel: A Study in Literary Design.* Philadelphia: Fortress, 1983.

Curtis, Bill, Stephen Rummage, and Daniel L. Akin. *Engaging Exposition.* Nashville: Broadman & Holman, 2011.

Davis, Elizabeth, ed. *A Higher Education: Baylor and the Vocation of a Christian University.* Waco, TX: Baylor University Press, 2012.

Deutschman, Alan. "Change or Die," Fast Company, May 2005. http://www.fastcompany.com/52717/change-or-die (accessed August 29, 2014).

Dittemore, Isabel. *He Leadeth Me.* Joplin, MO: College Press, 1998.

Duke, Robert W. *The Sermon as God's Word.* Nashville: Broadman & Holman, 1981.

Duvall, J. Scott, and J. Daniel Hays. *Grasping God's Word: A Hands-On Approach to Reading, Interpreting, and Applying the Bible.* 3rd ed. Grand Rapids: Zondervan, 2012.

Dyne, Linn Van, Soon Ang, and Christine Koh. "Development and Validation of the CQS: The Cultural Intelligence Scale." In *Handbook of Cultural Intelligence,* edited by Soon Ang and Linn Van Dyne, 16–38. Armonk, NY: M.E. Sharpe, 2008.

Edwards, J. Kent. *Deep Preaching: Creating Sermons that Go Beyond the Superficial.* Nashville: Broadman & Holman, 2009.

———. *Effective First-Person Biblical Preaching.* Grand Rapids: Zondervan, 2005.

Evans, Craig A. *Mark 8:27–16:20.* Word Biblical Commentary 34b. Dallas: Word, 2001.

Erdman, Chris. *Countdown to Sunday: A Daily Guide for Those Who Dare to Preach.* Grand Rapids: Brazos, 2007.

Eslinger, Richard. *The Web of Preaching: New Options in Homiletic Method.* Nashville: Abingdon, 2002.

Eswine, Zack. *Preaching to a Post-Everything World.* Grand Rapids: Baker, 2008.

Faur, J. "The Biblical Idea of Idolatry." *Jewish Quarterly Review* 69 (1978) 1–15.

Fee, Gordon D., and Stuart, Douglas. *How to Read the Bible for All Its Worth.* Grand Rapids: Zondervan, 1982.

———. *How to Read the Bible for All Its Worth.* 2nd ed. Grand Rapids: Zondervan, 1993.

———. *How to Read the Bible for All Its Worth.* 3rd ed. Grand Rapids: Zondervan, 2003.

Fensham, F. C. "The Burning of the Golden Calf and Ugarit." *Israel Exploration Journal* 16 (1966) 191–93.

Fitch, Alger M. *What the Bible Says About Preaching.* Joplin, MO: College Press, 1989.

Fleer, David, and Dave Bland. *Preaching the Eighth Century Prophets.* Abilene, TX: ACU Press, 2004.

Foster, Richard. *Life With God: Reading the Bible for Spiritual Transformation.* San Francisco: HarperOne, 2008.

Fraleigh, Douglas M., and Joseph S. Tuman. *Speak Up: An Illustrated Guide to Public Speaking.* Boston: Bedford/St. Martins, 2014.

Frankland, Dinelle. *His Story, Our Response: What the Bible Says About Worship.* Joplin, MO: College Press, 2008.

Friedman, Edwin H. *Generation to Generation: Family Process in Church and Synagogue.* New York: Guilford, 2011.

"Frosty the Snowman." December 19, 2006. www.youtube.com/watch?v=pmuJDmjq-xQ (accessed September 9, 2014).

Gaddy, C. Welton. *The Gift of Worship.* Nashville: Broadman, 1992.

Gardner, Howard. *Intelligence Reframed: Multiple Intelligences for the 21st Century.* New York: Basic, 1999.

Geisler, Norman, *To Understand the Bible Look for Jesus.* Grand Rapids: Baker, 1968.

George, Timothy. "Doctrinal Preaching." In *A Handbook of Contemporary Preaching,* edited by Michael Duduit, 93–102. Nashville: Broadman & Holman, 1992.

Giglio, Louie. "Moses, the Little Leader." North American Christian Convention Sermon. Phoenix: July 2004.

Grant, Reg. "Literary Structure in the Book of Ruth." *Bibliotheca Sacra* 148 (1991) 424–41.

Green, Joel B. "Luke-Acts, or Luke and Acts? A Reaffirmation of Narrative Unity." In *Reading Acts Today: Essays in Honour of Loveday C. A. Alexander,* edited by Steve Walton, Thomas E. Phillips, Lloyd K. Pietersen, and F. Scott Spencer, 101–19. Library of New Testament Studies 427. London: T & T Clark, 2011.

———. "Reading the Gospels and Acts as Narrative." In *Narrative Reading, Narrative Preaching,* edited by Joel B. Green and Michael Pasquarello III, 37–66. Grand Rapids: Baker, 2003.

———. "The (Re-)Turn to Narrative." In *Narrative Reading, Narrative Preaching,* edited by Joel B. Green and Michael Pasquarello III, 11–36. Grand Rapids: Baker Academic, 2003.

Greidanus, Sidney. *The Modern Preacher and the Ancient Text: Interpreting and Preaching Biblical Literature.* Grand Rapids: Eerdmans, 1988.

Hansen, Richard. "The Playful Preacher: Using Humor and Irony." In *The Art & Craft of Biblical Preaching: A Comprehensive Resource for Today's Communicators,* edited by Haddon Robinson and Craig Brian Larson, 210–213. Grand Rapids: Zondervan, 2005.

Hanson, Amy. *Baby Boomers and Beyond.* San Francisco: Jossey-Bass, 2010.

Hatina, Thomas R. *New Testament Theology and Its Quest for Meaning.* New York: Bloomsbury T & T Clark, 2013.

Heifetz, Ronald A., and Marty Linsky. *Leadership on the Line.* Boston: Harvard Business School Press, 2002.

Heisler, Greg. "The Expository Method." *Preaching* 23 (Jan–Feb 2008) 23–24.

———. *Spirit-Led Preaching.* Nashville: Broadman & Holman, 2007.

Hoffmeier, J. K. "Moses." In *International Standard Bible Encyclopedia,* edited by Geoffrey W. Bromiley, 3:2083–91. Rev. ed. Grand Rapids: Eerdmans, 1979–1988.

Holy Bible: New International Version. Textbook edition. Grand Rapids: Zondervan, 2011.

Hyers, Conrad. *And God Created Laughter: The Bible as Divine Comedy.* Atlanta: Westminster John Knox, 1987.

"I Love You." June 26, 2013. www.youtube.com/watch?v=FFlkQorzsyE (accessed September 2, 2014).

Jacks, G. Robert. *Just Say the Word!: Writing for the Ear.* Grand Rapids: Eerdmans, 1996.

Jones, J. K., and Mark Scott. *Letting the Text Win.* Joplin, MO: College Press, 2014.

Kaiser, Walter C., Jr., and Moises Silva. *Introduction to Biblical Hermeneutics*. 2nd ed. Grand Rapids: Zondervan, 2007.

Kauflin, Bob. *Worship Matters*. Wheaton, IL: Crossway, 2008.

Keener, Craig S. *Acts: An Exegetical Commentary (Introduction and 1:1–2:47)*. Vol. 1 of 4. Grand Rapids: Baker, 2012.

Kelly, J. N. D. *The Pastoral Epistles*. London: Continuum, 1963.

Key, A. F. "Traces of the Worship of the Mood God Sin Among the Early Israelites." *Journal of Biblical Literature* 84 (1965) 20–26.

Kidner, Derek. *Ezra & Nehemiah: A Introduction and Commentary*. Downers Grove, IL: IVP, 1979.

Kingsbury, Jack Dean. *Matthew as Story*. 2nd ed. Philadelphia: Fortress, 1988.

Knight, G. W. *The Pastoral Epistles: A Commentary on the Greek Text*. Grand Rapids: Eerdmans, 1992.

Koch, J.R. "The 119 Project: Who Wrote Psa 119?" http://www.the119project.com/#!who-wrote-Psa-119/c9z7 (accessed December 15, 2014).

Koessler, John. "Why All the Best Preachers are Theological." In *The Art and Craft of Biblical Preaching*, edited by Haddon Robinson and Craig Brian Larson, 241–46. Grand Rapids: Zondervan, 2005.

Köstenberger, Andreas J., and Richard D. Patterson. *Invitation to Biblical Interpretation: Exploring the Hermeneutical Triad of History, Literature, and Theology*. Grand Rapids: Kregel, 2011.

Kotter, John P. *A Force for Change: How Leadership Differs from Management*. New York: Free Press, 1990.

————. "What Leaders Really Do." *Harvard Business Review* (December 2001).

Kuruvilla, Abraham. *Privilege the Text*. Chicago: Moody, 2013.

Laertes, Diogenes. *Lives of Eminent Philosophers*. 2 vols. The Loeb Classical Library 184–185. Translated by R. D. Hicks. Cambridge: Harvard University Press, 1959.

Lakoff, George. *Don't Think of an Elephant! Know Your Values and Frame the Debate*. White River Junction, VT: Chelsea Green, 2004.

LeCureux, Jason T. *The Thematic Unity of the Book of the Twelve*. Sheffield: Sheffield Phoenix, 2012.

Lewy, I. "The Story of the Golden Calf Reanalysed." *Vetus Testamentum* 9 (1959) 318–322.

Lilley, J.P.U. "Joshua." In *New Bible Dictionary*, edited by D. R. W. Wood, 612. 3rd ed. Downers Grove, IL: InterVarsity, 1996.

Lischer, Richard. *A Theology of Preaching*. Nashville: Abingdon, 1981.

Loewenstamm, S. E. "The Making and Destruction of the Golden Calf." *Biblica* 48 (1967) 481–490.

————. "The Making and Destruction of the Golden Calf—A Rejoinder." *Biblica* 56 (1975) 330–343.

Long, Thomas G. *Beyond the Worship Wars: Building Vital and Faithful Worship*. Bethesda, MD: The Alban Institute, 2001.

————. *Preaching and the Literary Forms of the Bible*. Philadelphia: Fortress, 1989.

Longman, Tremper. *Literary Approaches to Biblical Interpretation*. Foundations of Contemporary Interpretation. Grand Rapids: Academie, 1987.

Lorde. "Royals." From the album *Pure Heroine*. September 27, 2013.

————. "Team." From the album *Pure Heroine*. September 27, 2013.

Loscalzo, Craig A. *Preaching Sermons That Connect*. Downers Grove, IL: IVP, 1992.

Lowery, Eugene. *The Homiletical Plot, Expanded Edition: The Sermon as Narrative Art Form.* Atlanta: Westminster John Knox, 2000.

Madison Park Christian Church. "Messages." Madison Park Christian Church. http://madisonparkchurch.com/sermon (accessed September 1, 2014).

———. "Who We Are: Our History." Madison Park Christian Church. http://madisonparkchurch.com/about/history (accessed September 1, 2014).

Malbon, Elizabeth Struthers. "Narrative Criticism: How Does the Story Mean?" In *Mark and Method,* edited by Janice Capel Anderson and Stephen D. Moore, 23–49. Minneapolis: Fortress, 1992.

Marshall, I. Howard. *New Testament Theology.* Downers Grove, IL: IVP, 2004.

Martin, Judith N., and Thomas K. Nakayama. *Experiencing Intercultural Communication.* New York: McGraw-Hill, 2011.

Massey, James Earl. *The Responsible Pulpit.* Anderson, IN: Warner, 1974.

Matera, Frank. *New Testament Theology.* Louisville: Westminster John Knox, 2007.

Matheny, Paul Duane; Clifford J. Green; and Marshall D. Johnson, eds. *The Young Bonhoeffer.* Translated by Mary C. Nebelsick. Minneapolis: Fortress, 2002.

Mathewson, Steven D. *The Art of Preaching Old Testament Narrative.* Grand Rapids: Baker, 2002.

McIntosh, Gary L. *One Church, Four Generations.* Grand Rapids: Baker, 2002.

McManus, Erwin. "Seizing Your Divine Moment." *Preaching Today* Tape #252.

McNeal, Reggie. *Missional Renaissance.* San Francisco: Jossey-Bass, 2009.

Melick, Richard R., and Shera Melick. *Teaching That Transforms: Facilitating Life Change through Adult Bible Teaching.* Nashville: Broadman & Holman, 2010.

Metaxas, Eric. *Bonhoeffer: Pastor, Martyr, Prophet, Spy.* Nashville: Thomas Nelson, 2010.

Metzger, B. M., et al. *The Making of the New Revised Standard Version of the Bible.* Grand Rapids: Eerdmans, 1991.

Mezirow, Jack. *Fostering Critical Reflection in Adulthood: A Guide to Transformative and Emancipatory Learning.* The Jossey-Bass Higher Education Series. 1st ed. San Francisco: Jossey-Bass, 1990.

———. *Learning as Transformation: Critical Perspectives on a Theory in Progress.* The Jossey-Bass Higher and Adult Education Series. 1st ed. San Francisco: Jossey-Bass, 2000.

———. *Transformative Dimensions of Adult Learning.* The Jossey-Bass Higher and Adult Education Series. 1st ed. San Francisco: Jossey-Bass, 1991.

Mezirow, Jack, and Edward W. Taylor. *Transformative Learning in Practice : Insights from Community, Workplace, and Higher Education.* 1st ed. San Francisco: Jossey-Bass, 2009.

Middleton, Richard J., and Brian J. Walsh. *Truth Is Stranger Than It Used to Be: Biblical Faith in a Postmodern Age.* Downers Grove, IL: IVP, 1995.

"The Mindset List for the Class of 2015." n.d. www.beloit.edu/mindset/previouslists/2015/. (accessed May 1, 2014)

Mohler, R. Albert, Jr. "A Theology of Preaching." In *A Handbook of Contemporary Preaching,* edited by Michael Duduit, 13–20. Nashville: Broadman & Holman, 1992.

Montgomery-Fate, Tom. *Beyond the White Noise: Mission in a Multicultural World.* St. Louis: Chalice, 1997.

Moore, Stephen D. *Literary Criticism and the Gospels: The Theoretical Challenge.* New Haven, CT: Yale University Press, 1992.

Noll, Mark. "The Bible, Baptists and the Challenge of Christian Higher Education." In *A Higher Education: Baylor and the Vocation of a Christian University*, edited by Elizabeth Davis, 95–111. Nashville: Baylor University Press, 2012.

O'Hair, Dan, Robert Stewart, and Hannah Rubenstein. *A Speaker's Guidebook: Text and Reference*. 5th ed. Boston: Bedford/St. Martins, 2012.

Oswalt, John N. "The Golden Calves and the Egyptian Concept of Deity." *Evangelical Quarterly* 45 (1973) 13–20.

Parsons, Michael C. *Acts*. Paideia Commentaries on the New Testament. Grand Rapids: Baker, 2008.

Pasquarello, Michael, III. *Christian Preaching*. Grand Rapids: Baker, 2006.

Peloubet, F. N. *Peloubet's Bible Dictionary*. Philadelphia: John C. Winston, 1947.

Perdue, L. G. "The Making and Destruction of the Golden Calf—A Reply." *Biblica* 54 (1973) 237–246.

Peterson, Eugene. *The Message*. Colorado Springs: NavPress, 2005.

Powell, Mark Allen. "Narrative Criticism: The Emergence of a Prominent Reading Strategy." In *Mark as Story: Retrospect and Prospect*, edited by Kelly Iverson and Christopher W. Skinner, 19–44. Atlanta: Society of Biblical Literature, 2011.

———. *What Is Narrative Criticism?* Minneapolis: Fortress, 1990.

Proctor, Matt, "A Beeline to the Cross: Preaching Christ Through All of Scripture." In *Preaching Through Tears*, edited by John D. Webb and Joseph C. Grana II, 103–122. Lincoln, NE: Lincoln Christian College and Seminary Alumni Association, 2000.

Quicke, Michael. *360-Degree Leadership: Preaching to Transform Congregations*. Grand Rapids: Baker, 2006.

Rainer, Thom S., and Jess W. Rainer. *The Millennials: Connecting to America's Largest Generation*. Nashville: Broadman & Holman, 2011.

Read, Ken E. *Created to Worship*. Joplin, MO: College Press, 2002.

Reid, Robert Stephen. "Exploring Preaching's Voices from Ex Cathedra to Exilic." In *Preaching the Eighth Century Prophets*, edited by David Fleer and David Bland, 135–168. Abilene, TX: ACU Press, 2004.

Rhoads, David. "Narrative Criticism: Practices and Prospects." In *Characterization in the Gospel: Reconceiving Narrative Criticism*, edited by David Rhoads and Kari Syreeni, 264–85. Journal for the Study of the New Testament Supplement Series 184. Sheffield: Sheffield Academic, 1999.

Rhoads, David, Joanna Dewey, and Donald Michie. *Mark as Story: An Introduction to the Narrative of a Gospel*. 3rd ed. Minneapolis: Fortress, 2012.

Richard, Ramesh. *Preparing Expository Sermons: A Seven-Step Method for Biblical Preaching*. Grand Rapids: Baker, 2001.

Roach, John. "'No Two Snowflakes the Same' Likely True, Research Reveals." National Geographic News. Last modified February 13, 2007. http://news.nationalgeographic. com/news/2007/02/070213-snowflake_2.html.

Robinson, Haddon. *Biblical Preaching*. 2nd ed. Grand Rapids: Baker, 2001.

———. *Biblical Preaching: The Development and Delivery of Expository Messages*. 3rd edition. Grand Rapids: Baker, 2014.

———. "Convictions of Biblical Preaching." In *The Art and Craft of Biblical Preaching*, edited by Haddon Robinson and Craig Brian Larson, 23–24. Grand Rapids: Zondervan, 2005.

Robinson, Haddon, and Craig Brian Larson, eds. *The Art and Craft of Biblical Preaching*. Grand Rapids: Zondervan, 2005.

Robinson, Haddon W., and Torrey W. Robinson. *It's All In How You Tell It*. Grand Rapids: Baker, 2003.

Rockstuhl, Thomas and Kok-Yee Ng. "The Effects of Cultural Intelligence on Interpersonal Trust in Multicultural Teams." In *Handbook of Cultural Intelligence: Theory, Measurement, and Applications*, edited by Soon Ang and Linn Van Dyne, 206–220. Armonk, NY: M.E. Sharpe, 2008.

Rogers, Everett M., and Thomas M. Steinfatt. *Intercultural Communication*. Long Grove, IL: Waveland, 1999.

Rosebrough, Thomas, and Ralph Leverett. "Faith and Transformational Teaching." In *Faith and Learning: A Handbook for Christian Higher Education*, edited by David S. Dockery, 475–498. Nashville: Broadman & Holman, 2012.

Russell, Walt. *Playing With Fire: How the Bible Ignites Change in Your Soul*. Colorado Springs: NavPress, 2000.

Ryken, Leland. *How to Read the Bible as Literature*. Grand Rapids: Academie, 1984.

Sackett, Chuck. "Somebody Cares." *Journal of the Evangelical Homiletics Society* 9, no. 1 (2009) 117–125.

———. Syllabus for Course PR660 *Leading from the Pulpit*. Lincoln, NE: Lincoln Christian Seminary, 2012.

Saffold, Guy. Coursepack for DMin. Course 880A *Theology of Leadership*. Deerfield: Trinity Evangelical Divinity School, 2007.

Sasson, J. M. "Bovine Symbolism in the Exodus Narrative." *Vetus Testamentum* 18 (1968) 380–87.

Saucy, Robert L. *Minding the Heart*. Grand Rapids: Kregel, 2013.

Schmidt, Frank L., and John E. Hunter. "Select on Intelligence." In *The Blackwell Handbook of Principals of Organizational Behavior*, edited by Edwin A. Locke, 3–14. Oxford: Blackwell, 2000.

Scott, Mark. "Biblical Preaching I." Class notes. Professors Dr. Haddon Robinson and Dr. Scott Wenig. Denver: Denver Seminary, Fall 1997.

Senn, Frank C. *Christian Worship and Its Cultural Setting*. Philadelphia: Fortress, 1983.

Shaw, Haydn. *Sticking Points*. Carol Stream, IL: Tyndale, 2013.

Skinner, Christopher W., and Kelly Iverson, eds. *Mark as Story: Retrospect and Prospect*. Atlanta: Society of Biblical Literature, 2011.

Smith, Robert, Jr. *Doctrine That Dances*. Nashville: Broadman & Holman, 2008.

Snodgrass, Klyne. *Stories with Intent*. Grand Rapids: Eerdmans, 2008.

Spencer, F. Scott. "The Narrative of Luke-Acts: Getting to Know the Savior God." In *Issues in Luke-Acts*, edited by Michael Pahl and Sean Adams, 121–46. Piscataway, NJ: Gorgias, 2012.

Stackhouse, Rochelle. "Music, Proclamation and Praise." In *Preaching in the Context of Worship*, edited by Ronald J. Allen and David M. Greenhaw, 89–98. St. Louis: Chalice, 2000.

Stott, John R. W. *Basic Christian Leadership*. Downers Grove, IL: IVP, 2002.

———. *Between Two Worlds: The Art of Preaching in the Twentieth Century*. Grand Rapids: Eerdmans, 1994.

———. "A Definition of Biblical Preaching." In *The Art and Craft of Biblical Preaching*, edited by Haddon Robinson and Craig Brian Larson, 24–28. Grand Rapids: Zondervan, 2005.

———. *The Message of 2 Timothy*. The Bible Speaks Today. Downers Grove, IL: IVP, 1973.

Sunukjian, Donald R. "The Homiletical Theory of Expository Preaching." PhD diss. Berkeley: University of California, 1974.

———. *Invitation to Biblical Preaching: Proclaiming Truth with Clarity and Relevance.* Grand Rapids: Kregel, 2007.

Talbert, Charles H. *Reading Acts: A Literary and Theological Commentary on the Acts of the Apostles.* Rev. ed. Reading the New Testament. Macon: Smyth & Helwys, 2005.

———. *Reading Luke: A Literary and Theological Commentary on the Third Gospel.* New York: Crossroad, 1988.

Tannehill, Robert C. *The Narrative Unity of Luke-Acts: A Literary Interpretation.* Vol. 1. Philadelphia: Fortress, 1986.

———. *The Narrative Unity of Luke-Acts: A Literary Interpretation.* Vol. 2. Philadelphia: Fortress, 1990.

Taylor, Charles. "Interculturalism or Multiculturalism?" *Philosophy and Social Criticism* 38 (2012) 413–423.

Taylor, Paul. *The Next America.* New York: PublicAffairs, 2014.

Teilhard de Chardin, Pierre. "Patient Trust." In *Hearts on Fire: Praying with Jesuits,* edited by Michael Harter, 102. Chicago: SJ Loyola, 2005.

Tenney, Merrill C., and Moisés Silva, eds. *The Zondervan Encyclopedia of the Bible.* Rev. ed. Grand Rapids: Zondervan, 2009.

Thatcher, Tom. "Anatomies of the Fourth Gospel: Past, Present, and Future Probes." In *Anatomies of Narrative Criticism: The Past, Present, and Futures of the Fourth Gospel as Literature,* edited by Tom Thatcher and Stephen D. Moore, 1–38. Atlanta: Society of Biblical Literature, 2008.

Thatcher, Tom, and Stephen D. Moore, eds. *Anatomies of Narrative Criticism: The Past, Present, and Futures of the Fourth Gospel as Literature.* Atlanta: Society of Biblical Literature, 2008.

Thorsen, D. A. D. *The Wesleyan Quadrilateral.* Grand Rapids: Zondervan, 1990.

Tidball, Derek. *Ministry By the Book.* Downers Grove, IL: IVP Academic, 2008.

Tornfelt, John. V. "Preaching and Leading: Mending A Fractured Relationship." *Evangelical Journal* 26 (2008) 1–4.

Trueblood, Elton. *Incendiary Fellowship.* New York: Harper and Row, 1967.

U2. "I Still Haven't Found What I'm Looking For." From the album *The Joshua Tree.* May 1987.

Underwood, Chuck. *The Generational Imperative: Understanding Generational Differences In The Workplace, Marketplace, And Living Room.* North Charleston, SC: Generational Imperative, 2007.

The United Church of Canada. "Defining Multicultural, Cross-Cultural, and Intercultural." http://www.united-church.ca/files/intercultural/multicultural-crosscultural-intercultural.pdf (accessed July 18 2014).

VanGemeren, Willem, ed. *New International Dictionary of Old Testament Theology & Exegesis.* Grand Rapids: Zondervan, 1997.

Venter, C. J. H. "Expository Preaching—A Re-Evaluation for Today." Paper delivered at the annual meeting of the Evangelical Homiletics Society. Chicago. October 17–19, 2002.

Vines, Jerry. *A Practical Guide to Sermon Preparation.* Chicago: Moody, 1985.

Walton, John H., Victor H. Matthews, and Mark W. Chavalas. *The IVP Bible Background Commentary: Old Testament.* Downers Grove, IL: IVP, 2000.

Way, R.J. "God, Names of." In *International Standard Bible Encyclopedia*, edited by Geoffrey W. Bromiley, 2:1264–68. Rev. ed. Grand Rapids, MI: Eerdmans, 1979–1988.

Webb, John D., and Joseph C. Grana II, eds. *Preaching Through Tears*. Lincoln, NE: Lincoln Christian College and Seminary Alumni Association, 2000.

Webber, Robert E. *Worship is a Verb*. Peabody: Hendrickson, 1992.

Whitney, Donald. *Spiritual Disciplines for the Christian Life*. Colorado Springs: NavPress, 1991.

Wilson, Seth, and Lynn Gardner. *Learning from God's Word*. Joplin, MO: College Press, 1989.

Wiersbe, Warren W. *Real Worship*. Grand Rapids: Baker, 2000.

Whedbee, William J. *The Bible and the Comic Vision*. Minneapolis: Fortress, 2002.

Wilhoit, James C., and Leland Ryken. *Effective Bible Teaching*. 2nd ed. Grand Rapids: Baker, 2012.

Willhite, Keith, and Scott M. Gibson. *The Big Idea of Biblical Preaching: Connecting the Bible to People*. Grand Rapids: Baker, 1999.

Wilt, Dan. "Is It Too Loud? Worship Accompaniment vs. Worship Immersion Culture." Last modified July 8, 2014. www.danwilt.com/is-it-too-loud-worship-accompaniment-vs-worship-immersion-culture.

Witherington, Ben, III. *The Acts of the Apostles: A Socio Rhetorical Commentary*. Grand Rapids: Eerdmans, 1998.

———. *Letters and Homilies for Hellenized Christians: Volume 1, A Socio-Rhetorical Commentary on Titus, 1–2 Timothy and 1–3 John*. Downers Grove, IL: IVP, 2006.

Wren, Brian. *Praying Twice: The Music and Words of Congregational Song*. Louisville: Wesminster John Knox, 2000.

Wright, N. T. *The New Testament and the People of God*. Philadelphia: Fortress, 1992.

———. *Surprised by Hope*. New York: HarperOne, 2008.

Yoder, June Allman, Marlene Kropf, and Rebecca Slough. *Preparing Sunday Dinner: A Collaborative Approach to Worship and Preaching*. Scottdale, PA: Herald, 2005.